To Laura,

Wishing you all the best in your endeavors... you're never too old to go after your dreams! Remember you're born unstopp[able]: Fabulous... Making you Unstoppable

Stay Unstoppable
Anne Bismark

The *Journey* to *ME*

Empowering You to Live a Life of Unstoppable Success

Ann Rusnak

BALBOA PRESS
A DIVISION OF HAY HOUSE

Copyright © 2016 Ann Rusnak.

Editing: TL Champion, Marnie L. Pehrson
Cover Design: Alison Jerry
Proofreading: Stacey Hall
Photographer: Linda Ford

All rights reserved. No part of this book may be used or reproduced by any means, graphic, electronic, or mechanical, including photocopying, recording, taping or by any information storage retrieval system without the written permission of the author except in the case of brief quotations embodied in critical articles and reviews.

Balboa Press books may be ordered through booksellers or by contacting:

Balboa Press
A Division of Hay House
1663 Liberty Drive
Bloomington, IN 47403
www.balboapress.com
1 (877) 407-4847

Because of the dynamic nature of the Internet, any web addresses or links contained in this book may have changed since publication and may no longer be valid. The views expressed in this work are solely those of the author and do not necessarily reflect the views of the publisher, and the publisher hereby disclaims any responsibility for them.

The author of this book does not dispense medical advice or prescribe the use of any technique as a form of treatment for physical, emotional, or medical problems without the advice of a physician, either directly or indirectly. The intent of the author is only to offer information of a general nature to help you in your quest for emotional and spiritual well-being. In the event you use any of the information in this book for yourself, which is your constitutional right, the author and the publisher assume no responsibility for your actions.

Any people depicted in stock imagery provided by Thinkstock are models,
and such images are being used for illustrative purposes only.
Certain stock imagery © Thinkstock.

Print information available on the last page.

ISBN: 978-1-5043-8961-7 (sc)
ISBN: 978-1-5043-8963-1 (hc)
ISBN: 978-1-5043-8962-4 (e)

Library of Congress Control Number: 2017916542

Balboa Press rev. date: 07/09/2018

This book is dedicated to my husband, Michael, who saw the good in me way before I did. Thank you for staying by me during all the good and bad times. Your unconditional love and positive emotional support has given me the strength and courage to boldly step into my Magical Essence. To my eldest daughter, Chantal, I love watching you live your dream! To my youngest daughter, Allyce, you inspired the promise I made to God not knowing it would lead to the road of breaking the cycle of abuse in our family. I'm so proud of both of you. Continue to follow your hearts. To my granddaughter, Lexie. Stay Unstoppable. Don't listen to anybody who says you can't live your dreams. Enjoy life, smile, love and be happy.

In memory of my grandmother Caroline Kowalski.

CONTENTS

Foreword ix
An Ancient Legend: Finding the Secret of Success, ... xi
Introduction xiii

Chapter 1   The Promise 1
Chapter 2   Storm of Worthlessness 8
Chapter 3   Step 1 - All Journeys Start with Hope 17
Chapter 4   Seduction at Harbor Blame 24
Chapter 5   Step 2 - The Strait of Lost Dreams 31
Chapter 6   A Special Compass for a Magical Adventure 41
Chapter 7   Step 3 - Island of Forgiveness 45
Chapter 8   Tropical Storm Guilt 52
Chapter 9   Step 4 - Island of Gratitude 57
Chapter 10   Step 5 - Island of Courage 65
Chapter 11   Step 6 - Island of Trust & Faith 75
Chapter 12   The Dreaded Pirates, Doubt and Fear 84
Chapter 13   Step 7 - Island of Self-Empowerment 91
Chapter 14   God's Sake, Follow Your Heart 98
Chapter 15   A New Legacy Begins 104

Marie's 21 Affirmations for Unstoppable Success 109
Marie's Morning and Nightly Transforming Routine 111
About Ann Rusnak 115
Acknowledgements 117

FOREWORD

by DeLores Pressley

Life is a journey and sometimes that journey can be great or sometimes it can be challenging. This book is meant to assist every part of your life's journey.

I have known Ann Rusnak for many years. She has experienced challenges in her life, but the beauty is that she is helping others by sharing her journey. This book will open your eyes to many of life's challenges and situations, and most importantly it provides you strategies and techniques to navigate your journey. It is a life map to the shortcuts you can take on your journey through these situations.

The Journey to ME will help you understand your worth, take powerful action and be unstoppable. Many times, because of society's norms, women (and some men) do not realize their value and allow these cultural stereotypes to determine their self-worth. Through this story, Ann demonstrates how extreme success is possible for all. She has provided additional tools to this book such as; the "Unstoppable Success Kit", videos and audios that you can use to advance you to success.

At times, going through life can be like climbing a mountain. Family and friends may not support you, and make the climb more challenging. Use this book to keep going, to "tell your truth" and be the authentic masterpiece that God has created you to be.

If someone shows you how to do something and you try and try but just can't quite get it like they can, that does not mean that there is something wrong with you. So, stop trying to live up to their expectations. This book will show you how to do it in your own way.

I have traveled the world as an International Motivational Speaker, Author and Life Coach and have read many books. This is one book that I plan to keep near me and use as a reference when I coach women because I like to introduce people to the tools that will help renew their faith, develop strategic plans and achieve ultimate success.

This book one of those great tools to use for yourself or to help someone else. If you haven't personally gone through a life challenge, you will at some point because "life happens". When life throws obstacles in your way, Ann Rusnak has given you answers on how to handle them. It's a "must read" book that can be used to take inspired actions on your life's journey.

Dr. DeLores Pressley
DeLoresPressley.com

Motivational Speaker, Founder and Principal of DeLores Pressley Worldwide and the "Born Successful Institute."

Author of "Clean out the Closets of Your Life" *and* "Believe in the Power of You."

AN ANCIENT LEGEND:

Finding the Secret of Success, Prosperity & Happiness

According to an ancient legend, a group of wise men were disturbed when they saw how humankind abused its wisdom. They decided to hide the secret of success and happiness where no one would ever again find it. But, where? The chief of the wise men called a council to decide.

One wise man said, "We will bury the secret of success and happiness in the dark depths of the Earth."

The chief of wise men thought about it for a while then responded, "No, that won't work. Humans will dig deep down into the Earth to find it."

A second wise man proposed, "We will sink the secret of success and happiness into the deepest ocean."

The chief thought about it for some time and then responded, "No, that won't work either. People will surely dive into the depths to find it."

Another wise man suggested, "We will hide it on top of the highest mountain."

Again, the chief rejected the idea after considering it and said, "Humans will certainly climb the highest mountain to find it."

He continued, "Here is what we will do. We will hide the secret of success and happiness deep inside every individual. They will *never* think to look for it there."

And to this day, people continue their search across the Earth digging, diving, and climbing in search of something they already possess within themselves.

~*Author Unknown

Each one of us already possesses the resources we need to be tremendously successful. We simply need to develop these gifts by becoming more of who we really are to discover the treasures in our heart. That's the secret of success and happiness.

~ Ann Rusnak

*Someone shared this story with me decades ago. It became a pivotal point in my recovery from emotional abuse in helping me restore and connect with my authentic self.

INTRODUCTION

by Ann Rusnak

Currently, women experience more freedom, opportunity and control over their lives than at any other time in history, thanks to the positive progress in changing attitudes and beliefs.

Yet our society still sends out unrealistic messages of what a woman is "supposed to" be and do. Because of these conflicting messages, many women still don't value their selves. They don't know their infinite worth and the value they bring to the world around them.

A woman may feel she's missing out on life if she is not in a relationship or has not been a mother. She can feel undervalued because she thinks she is not as flawless as a model on a magazine cover. She may also feel she is being judged by others when she chooses to have a career rather than stay home to care for her children all day. Or, she may feel she is being judged if she does choose to stay home and care for her children instead of pursuing a career.

This leaves many women feeling emotionally damaged, frustrated and unfulfilled. Even with all the progress women have made, these women have not received the message: be true to yourself and pursue the life you envision.

Yes, we've come a long way, but we as women, still have a long way to go until we arrive at the point where we believe in ourselves and see our worth as a precious gift to the world. Because, it takes a lot of courage to be yourself, many women need the right kind of tools and encouragement to do just that.

Many self-help and personal growth books are written by men from the male perspective, encouraging everyone to follow their dreams. They often leave out the key ingredient many women need: a focus on self-worth. But how does a woman develop a sense of self-worth?

Another challenge for women on the path to self-empowerment includes the type of self-help books written from the perspective of co-dependence. A co-dependent relationship can be associated with passivity and feelings of shame, low self-worth, or insecurity because a co-dependent person will frequently sacrifice their own personal needs and identity to meet the needs of another, often a partner, spouse or family member. These books are often written by doctors and therapists with a clinical point of view.

Instead of the same old "how-to" self-help format, this transformational novel, you ae reading now tells a story to break through the mind's defenses, the defenses which blocks one's desire to change.

Your current beliefs feel comfortable even if they don't support the change you want to make. Most self-help books use facts and statistics as a way to convince the mind to change these long-held beliefs. Instead, though, the mind goes into 'protection' mode, because it perceives these new facts as threats.

Even if the facts are true, they don't address the emotional attachment your mind has to it's current belief system. Change happens at the emotional level first.

Think of a time you enjoyed watching a movie, with a plot that wasn't realistic. You become engrossed in the storyline and characters.

Your mind didn't feel threaten because it knew it wasn't real and it relaxed its beliefs so you could go along with the implausible story.

This is why I chose to wrap my message of personal empowerment within a story format. I want your mind to feel as comfortable as possible so it will allow you to make the change with least resistance.

In *The Journey to ME*, you will travel with Marie, who embarks on an unexpected, yet wondrous adventure. She starts her journey with doubt, following society's script for her life, and discovers an opportunity to uncover her true potential and the courage to embrace her inner ME.

Marie meets various mentors along the way. They help her believe in herself, to follow her inner guidance and discover her dreams. In the process, she creates a new legacy for her daughter.

My name is Ann Rusnak and I grew up being told everything about me was wrong, including the fact that I was born a girl. But a voice deep inside kept pushing me, urging and guiding me to follow my dreams.

In pursuit of those dreams, I overcame emotional and religious abuse, breaking the abuse cycle to create a new legacy for myself and future generations.

As a result, I now live a fantastic life, love myself unconditionally, and healed a damaged relationship with my eldest daughter. I raised my youngest daughter with the confidence to feel comfortable being herself.

I want to impart wisdom and knowledge from years of experience by empowering other women to see and accept their self-worth and the value they bring into the world.

This book is written by a woman for women. I chose to write this book to give women permission to embrace their self-worth and follow their hearts. And most importantly, the way to trust their inner voice and follow their dreams.

Know you are a worthy person just because you exist, as a creation in God's image.

What benefits does *The Journey to ME* offer the reader?

It offers the "7 Steps of the Unstoppable Success System" to help you realize and discover:

- How the secret to personal success is already within you.
- A belief in you true potential
- You are made in God's image and are a gift to the world
- How to love and accept yourself
- You need to quit people-pleasing and put your needs first so can you gain a sense of who you are as an individual.
- Why fear and doubt are the thieves of your destiny *(and how to render them ineffective)*

- How to fulfill that deep longing for living up to your potential by using your talents and gifts
- By being yourself, you can make a positive difference in the world
- No matter what happened in the past, you can still do amazing things and live a great life
- How to leave a legacy of confidence for your children

SPECIAL GIFT FOR YOU!

Congratulations on opening and reading this book. You have taken the first step in realizing your dreams.

My passion is to empower you to believe in yourself, your value and you heart-felt dreams. It's time to use your God-given potential to positively change the world by living the life you richly deserve!

To help you stay on the path to having it all, I created this gift exclusively for you, your "Unstoppable Success Kit."

Imagine taking just five minutes a day to use the tools in this *kit (affirmation video, audio and Anchor ME ™ playbook)* to easily transform your old limiting thoughts to ones that empower you to "play it big".

Go to: **www.TheJourneytoMeGift.com** to download your "Unstoppable Success Kit: A Simple and Easy Way to Attract Success in Less Than 5 Minutes A Day."

MORE GIFTS FOR YOU…

A *treasure hunt* awaits you… Sprinkled throughout this book, you'll find several treasure items to add to your Success Kit. Keep on reading and watch for these gems.

CHAPTER 1

The Promise

Marie begins to tremble. It feels like her insides are tearing apart. Her mind fragments into tiny pieces. She can't tell where she is as she watches something devour the dim lighting.

She knows something is wrong… very wrong.

The recesses of her mind darken, hiding any sense of the life she knows. Her out-stretched arms to feel the way through the darkness. She stumbles and trips falling deeper into the unknown.

Drifting in and out of consciousness, chaos swirls through her mind and she continues reaching, trying to grab onto anything stable. She desperately wants to feel safe and secure again.

Something in this black void reaches out and grabs her throat. She feels a pressure growing tighter, choking out any remaining sense of reality. She's not sure she can tell the difference between real or fantasy any more.

Marie gasps for air. She craves a life of inner peace and tries to pull herself out of the abyss. A loud noise outside jolts her from her nightmarish sleep. The remnants leave her mind foggy and for a brief instance she wonders where she is.

She sits upright in bed and is bathed in sunlight. She realizes she couldn't ask for a truer friend than Barb, who offered her the use of her Georgia coast beach front cottage while she and her father are away.

Marie's daughter, Elizabeth, is at summer camp, making this the perfect opportunity to take time for herself. She needs to gather her thoughts after her recent decision to separate from her husband, Lloyd.

Marie shakes herself free of the leftover nightmarish feelings and heads for the bathroom to take a shower.

She steps into the spa-like enclosure and lets the warm pulsating water from various sprays massage away the edgy moments of her dream. The comforting waters from the ceiling sprays feel like a gentle rain. She enjoys the smooth-flowing streams running down her back as it rinses the shampoo out of her shoulder length brunette hair.

Marie feels her family's disappointment weighing heavily upon her. She still finds it frustrating that they practically blame *her* for the discord of her eleven-year marriage. As the warm water drizzles down her slim body, she hears her parents' voices echoing in her head, telling her she's behaving in a selfish way. She replays their accusing tone as they tell her she's only thinking about herself and not her daughter.

Would they understand if she told them a divorce will protect Elizabeth from a father who berates her? That a divorce will allow Marie to keep a promise she made to God? Probably not. From past experience, any explanation would prove futile, because they only see Lloyd in the good husband, father, and "provider" role. She realizes this is partly her fault for not being honest with them about his behavior over the years.

⟨∞⟩

Marie thinks back to how she thought Lloyd loved her. He seemed to say and do all the right things to make her feel special. In his way, he did, which also meant he expected her to meet his ideals of perfection. His subtle innuendos made it clear that anything less reflected badly on him. Lord knows she tried to live up to the ideals of the perfect wife and mother. But, no matter how hard she tried, no matter how well she did, she always fell short of meeting his impossible expectations. Lloyd constantly embarrassed and humiliated Marie.

It didn't take long for the bliss of her marriage to fade. She talked to Lloyd about this, suggesting they go to counseling or marriage therapy. He refused.

His lack of respect reminded her of her relationship with her parents. She did her best to create the persona of the perfect couple with a nice home, new cars, and yearly vacations. To anybody looking from the outside, their family appeared picture-perfect.

He thought their marriage needed a child to complete the picture. The thought of raising a daughter made Marie's heart jump with happiness. *Maybe a child will make things better*, she thought.

Marie made a promise to God. If He gave her a daughter, she promised to honor how precious He made her. She would protect her daughter, nurture her dreams and love her unconditionally. She wanted to spare her the experience of growing up feeling *worthless*.

But months ago, Marie witnessed her verbally abusive husband do the same thing to their daughter. When she saw how his words affected Elizabeth, she knew something needed to change. It opened Marie's eyes to the emotional cruelty Lloyd had dealt out to her on a regular basis.

She decided to talk to a lawyer to discuss her options.

Marie felt relief knowing her daughter would be away from him. She realized she could use a break too, so she gladly accepted Barb's invitation to stay at her place in Paradise Cove. Barb told her the solitude would help her gain clarity about the direction of her life. Barb was right!

Marie's thoughts come back to the present. She grabs a towel to dry off and wonders, "I really wish I knew the secret to finding everlasting happiness. Why does it always seem just out of reach? Is it possible to keep my promise *and* pursue my dreams?"

Marie sighs with a glimmer of hope that perhaps one day, she will find answers to those question. She heads downstairs to the kitchen and turns on the coffee maker.

The fresh aroma of coffee fills the kitchen while Marie spreads cream cheese on her warm toasted bagel. She pours a cup of coffee and walks outside to sit on the deck. A flock of seagulls flies overhead to greet her. She watches the birds fly away and then closes her eyes listening intently to the sound of ocean waves. She wishes her troubles could wash away with the waves, leaving her with an opportunity for a fresh, new life.

Her cell phone rings, interrupting her thoughts. She sees her friend's name on the caller I.D.

"Hello, Barb," Marie answers.

"Good morning," Barb replies, "Meet me at Café Joes down by the dock in thirty minutes for a surprise."

"Barb, are you all right?"

"Everything is fine, Marie."

"I thought you and your father left for your annual father-daughter adventure yesterday morning?"

"We did. But I got a brilliant idea. My dad thought we should share it with you. No more questions. I'll see you shortly."

Excitement fills Marie's senses and she wonders what would possibly make them turn the sailboat around. She retreats inside, turns off the coffee maker, refreshes her sunscreen, puts on her walking shoes and heads out the door.

Marie follows the sandy path flanked by sea oats and honeysuckle-covered fences. The fragrant blossoms escort her on her walk until the path meets the main street sidewalk.

The specialty shops along the street fill with the first of the season's tourists. Looking through the windows, she can see their excited faces when they discover a special treasure. Her own excitement grows when she catches sight of Café Joes. Marie feels honored to finally meet Barb's father.

Barb has shared her father's wisdom with her over the years, especially how he filled his dream of entrepreneurship. She has recounted stories about how he started his business twenty-five years ago. How the success of his company provided a good living for seventy-five employees, and enabled him to follow his other passion, sailing.

Over the years, Barb's father created a business environment that encourages his employees to embrace their natural abilities. Barb told Marie he strongly believes following a dream honors one's authentic self.

Barb shared how her parents taught her to embrace her gifts and personality and how this same encouragement instills a burning desire in people, giving them an inner drive to fully engage in discovering their potential, to achieve their heart's desire and live the life they richly deserve.

Barb's father told her since she was a child that she was born *unstoppable*. He says that when people stop following their dreams, they disconnect from their authentic selves. This can lead to a life of frustration, anxiety and depression leaving one feeling as if something is missing.

Marie never heard those words of encouragement from her parents. She couldn't imagine her parents teaching her to reach for the sky!

Marie crosses the street to the café with pleasant memories of previous visits she enjoyed with Barb and both their daughters.

Marie notices the café looks a little different today. Something about the way the sunlight bathes the row of buildings catches her eye. She takes a seat at an outside table overlooking the Sound. She orders a cup of coffee and sips it slowly while thinking about the first time she met Barb.

※

Nine years ago, Marie and Lloyd moved to an upscale gated community in their city. He generated a good income at the brokerage firm and decided that with a baby on the way, they needed a bigger home that would reflect his success.

With the move and impending birth of Elizabeth, Lloyd felt things would improve if Marie quit her teaching job. He made plenty of money and decided she didn't need to work.

Marie felt so happy with her baby girl that it distracted her from Lloyd's overbearing nature. Elizabeth turned nine months old when Marie enrolled her in swimming lessons offered at the club house. Barb also signed up her one-year-old daughter, McKenzie, for lessons. She and Barb hit it off and Marie enjoyed having someone to share the ups and downs of motherhood. She no longer felt isolated since Lloyd rarely wanted to hear about her day.

Marie's parents made it clear they did not approve of her relationship with Barb. They believe Barb's influence and grandiose ideas of "following your dreams," filled their daughter's mind with unrealistic expectations. They often blamed Barb for Marie's marriage difficulties and they didn't approve of the growing friendship between their granddaughter and McKenzie.

※

The clinking sound of chimes from a nearby shop, causes Marie to abandon her thoughts. Her attention shifts to the sun's reflection on the rippling waters and she catches herself smiling at the dancing jewel effect it creates.

She notices a flock of noisy sea gulls escorting a beautiful sailboat entering the inlet. The white sails gleam in the bright sun, giving it an ethereal glow. *This must be Barb and her father pulling in, she thinks to herself.*

As Barb and the elderly gentleman help tie the boat up to the dock, Marie catches the words *"Magical Essence"* painted in black lettering on the stern. She watches Barb and her father walk down the dock toward the café.

Barb's frosted, layered blond hair dances loosely in the breeze. The form-fitting blue polo and khaki shorts compliment her athletic body. When Marie waves to her, they both start briskly walking towards each other until they meet and exchange hugs.

Shortly afterwards, the elderly gentleman reaches them.

"Marie, meet my father, captain of the Magical Essence," Barb announces.

"Pleasure to meet you," Marie replies.

"Pleasure to meet you, Marie. Call me Captain T. I bet you're busting at the seams wondering what this is all about."

"You certainly read my mind, Captain T."

"Since Barb came up with this great idea, I'll let her share it over lunch. I'm starving," he says tipping his navy captain's hat forward and revealing a lock of his silver hair. The lanky gentleman smiles at her, and as his deep blue eyes meet hers, it feels as if he can read her soul.

The three of them head to Café Joes and sit at a bistro table. The waitress refreshes Marie's coffee and places a cup in front of Barb and her father. While they wait for lunch, Barb starts the conversation.

"A little voice kept nagging at me to come back and get you. I want you to join us on our trip! When I shared my thoughts with my father, he agreed."

Captain T chimes in, "I taught my children to follow their intuition. Since Barb's was practically screaming at her, we decided to turn the boat around!"

Marie almost drops the coffee cup in her hands. "I hate to intrude on your trip," she responds.

Captain T says, "This is *not* an intrusion. Believe me, you only turn around a 174-foot yacht headed to the Bahamas for a good reason. You look like good reason to me," he says with a smile. "It would be an *honor* for you to join us."

"So… what do you think?" Barb asks.

Captain T senses hesitation in Marie, so he asks her to close her eyes. He says, "Before you tell us all the reasons you shouldn't, take a deep breath and let it out. Clear all your thoughts and tell me, what is your heart telling you to do? Just listen."

With her eyes shut, Marie replies with a smile forming, "It's telling me to go… I really want to go. I've always wanted to go to the Bahamas."

She opens her eyes when Barb yells out, "Well, let's go!" and The Captain quickly seconds the motion. He tells Marie to go back to the house, pack a bag and meet them at the boat in an hour.

Marie's feet barely touch the ground as she walks back to the beach house. She quickly gathers some items, texts her daughter about the change in plans and says she'll call her later that evening.

Within minutes, she meets Barb and the Captain in the harbor and boards the Magical Essence. Marie can't contain her excitement when they release the boat from the dock and hoist the sails as they leave the harbor. She experiences an odd feeling that she's about to embark on the adventure of a lifetime.

CHAPTER 2

Storm of Worthlessness

The wind playfully weaves through Marie's shoulder-length brown hair while she raises her face to greet the warmth of the sun. This almost feels like a dream.

One of the ship's crew brings a pitcher of ice tea and three frosted glasses on a tray with some chips and salsa.

The cool liquid clinks the ice cubes against the glass while the ocean waves lap against the side of the boat. Marie presses the glass to her lips and the refreshing beverage quenches her thirst.

She remarks, "Now I can see why Barb enjoys sailing so much."

As their journey begins, a pair of dolphins appear alongside the boat, jumping in and out of the water, as if to dare the Magical Essence to a race.

Captain T turns to Marie and says, "Enjoying yourself?"

"Oh, yes! Thanks so much for inviting me."

"You're welcome, Marie. I'll leave you two alone while I go do my captain thing. Enjoy the refreshments, but don't get too full. We'll be dining on smoked salmon with fresh grilled vegetables."

"Sounds wonderful," Marie replies.

Marie and Barb enjoy the rest of the afternoon lounging on the deck. Marie can't remember the last time she allowed herself to just relax, be in the moment, and enjoy something as simple as the sun on her back and the breeze caressing her skin.

As the afternoon wears on and the sun begins to descend closer to the horizon, the crew sets up the outdoor dining area for the sumptuous feast.

"The table looks lovely," Marie comments. "And everything looks and smells wonderful. I can't believe how hungry I am."

"Yep, the sea air and sunshine can work up a hearty appetite," Barb replies.

After Marie fills her plate, she tales a bite and says, "Mmmmm, my compliments to the chef," as she savors another bite of fish.

"The salmon practically melts in my mouth. Everything is *delicious*," She adds after taking a sip of her drink.

"Glad you enjoyed dinner," the Captain remarks.

The crew begins to clear the plates when Barb says, "Who wants a treat? Sipping margaritas while watching the sunset will be perfect. Is anybody else interested?"

Marie and the Captain say simultaneously, "Margaritas sound great." They look at each other and chuckle.

Barb returns with a pitcher of drinks and three glasses.

They watch the sun slowly lower behind the horizon, painting the sky above in hues of orange and purple. Then evening releases the sun's masterpiece and darkens the set for the night show. One by one the stars make their appearance.

Marie leans back in the lounge chair in awe of the brightness above her. "Wow, look at the sky so full of stars. This wonderful boat, a great dinner, margaritas, and perfect view feels like such a luxury," she says dreamily. "Can you imagine living life like this every day?"

The Captain answers by saying, "Yes Marie, life is meant to be *enjoyed*. You can live every day like this *if you choose*."

"What???" Marie answers with skepticism in her voice.

Captain T continues, "We are all born deserving to live a richly beautiful life. You included."

"Well, I don't know about *deserve*. It is a nice thought, though," Marie says, but, inside she thinks *if he only knew the real me, he wouldn't say that. I'm far from deserving.*"

She continues the conversation, "I know my daughter, Elizabeth *deserves* to enjoy this kind of life... even better, she deserves all her heart's desires."

Marie starts thinking about how Lloyd has given their daughter a luxurious lifestyle. Something she can't provide on a teacher's salary, if she could even find a job.

What Captain T says next jolts her back to reality. "Tell me Marie, why do you think Elizabeth deserves her heart's desires, but not you?"

The question catches Marie off guard and she begins to stammer. "Well… umm, she just does. My parents wanted me to be my best, they pushed me, encouraged me. I just *failed*. I let my husband down too. Some of us are meant to live our dreams, others, like me… well… when you think about it, many people envy my life."

"Marie, no one comes into the world believing they can't live their dreams. You *learn* to believe this about yourself," Captain T says.

"Elizabeth is not me. She's smart, fun, loving and talented. She always does her best. Lord knows, I tried, but I just can't please everyone," Marie says with her voice breaking while she tries to hold back the tears welling in her eyes.

"I feel like I've failed as a wife, mother and daughter… I just want them to be proud of me, but no one is."

She tries to keep her composure, but finds herself breaking down hysterically, sobbing uncontrollably. She can barely speak between the sobs. While attempting to catch her breath, she notices Captain T raising he eyebrows and Barb's eyes growing wider. Marie thinks, *"Oh no… now I did it."*

But before she could say anything, Barb breaks the silence by saying, "Oh my gosh Marie, are you alright? I've never seen you so upset."

Between sobs, Marie says to Barb, "Do you remember the day you came over to help me prep for the neighborhood party?"

"Yes. Isn't that the same day Elizabeth found out she won the summer art camp scholarship?" Barb inquires.

"Correct," Marie replies as she tries to compose herself.

She looks over at Barb's father and continues, "Captain T, Elizabeth was *so* happy that day. She came running into the house screaming 'I did it, I did it' waving a piece of paper with excitement and pride beaming from her face."

Marie continues, "Elizabeth plays the violin at the Pennington Elementary School of the Arts. The school offered scholarships to the Center of the Arts summer camp for several categories this year. The top three who improved the most in their field performance had a chance to win."

"Are you talking about the goals the girls set so they could go to summer camp together?" Captain T asks her.

"Yes," Marie replies.

"Ahhh, I remember," said Captain T. "My granddaughter got hers for dance. She loves to dance."

"Yes, Dad she does," Barb agrees continuing the story. "The girls practiced together for hours and hours. McKenzie did her dance moves while Elizabeth played the violin."

Marie says, "I wanted to celebrate by doing something special for Elizabeth by making her favorite dinner and dessert. Then I asked if she wanted anything else."

Barb starts laughing, "Both girls shouted, 'We want to get our nails done'."

"Elizabeth enjoyed the manicure for her birthday and they wanted another one," Marie adds. "They were giggling and shouting gleefully when Lloyd came home from work asking what the commotion was about. Elizabeth ran over to him excitingly waving her scholarship certificate, screaming 'Daddy, Daddy, I get to go to summer art camp.'

"Lloyd congratulated her while reading the certificate and then responded in an irritating tone, 'Wait, you only made second chair? Not first chair?'"

"No, Daddy," Elizabeth responded with the excitement leaving her voice.

Lloyd told her, 'If you practice harder at camp *you can still make first chair*. The Johnson's never settle for second place. No daughter of mine should ever settle for second place.' Elizabeth's excitement faded and she ran upstairs to her room, tears streaming down her cheeks.

"It upset me to see her crying. His bullying spoiled the whole thing! Something came over me. I finally got the courage to tell him off for the first time in our 11-year marriage.

"I said, 'Lloyd, how could you? Didn't you see the happiness on her face and hear the excitement in her voice? Why did you want to burst her bubble? Her goal was summer camp, not first chair. She worked *hard* to get it'.

"Then he tells me she *should be* disappointed not making first chair and it's *my fault* for setting low expectations in the first place. He said,

'How is she going to live up to her potential if you coddle her? What an embarrassment it will be for me to tell everyone she's *second chair* instead of first. What kind of mother accepts mediocrity for their children?'"

"I asked him to apologize and he said, 'There was nothing to apologize for. You're the one making a big deal out of this, being too sensitive and passing these traits on to Elizabeth. After all, I did congratulate her.'"

"I told him she deserved to be treated better and he shook his head in disgust and said, 'It is your fault for blowing everything out of proportion again.' He never noticed the disappointment his words caused her. I watched her spirit go dim. Boy, could I relate to her feelings. It was just like listening to my own parents."

"I know, Marie," Barb says. "McKenzie told me how Elizabeth cried after he dropped her off at camp. Lloyd was still going on about what a disappointment she was. It's why I offered you the use of my beach home. I thought some time away from Lloyd you might help you realize the effect of his behavior. But something told me you needed more than a break, you needed a long vacation to gain clarity on what to do next. So, we came back for you."

Marie looks intently at Barb and says with lips trembling, "Do you remember what you whispered to me when you left my house?"

"Yes, do you?"

"You told me I deserve better treatment too," Marie replies.

Tears form in Marie's eyes, "I will break my promise to God if I stay with Lloyd. I can't undo any humiliation Elizabeth received from her father, but I can stop it from ever happening again. He gave her the same message I received growing up. She'll come to believe the same thing about herself over time. That she's not *good enough*."

Marie says hopefully… "I want to believe I deserve a better life."

"Marie, the first phase in changing your situation begins with awareness," Captain T says. "You took an important step in realizing you deserve a rich fulfilling life just as we all do."

Marie wipes the tears from her eyes and releases a heavy sigh.

"I'm sorry for losing it." Marie says." I think I'd like to retire early. I'm exhausted after today's excitement and the restless sleep I experienced last night."

"Of course," Barb and her father say in unison.

"No apology necessary," says Captain T.

Barb adds, "I completely understand. Get a good night's rest and pleasant dreams."

"Good night, Barb. Good night, Captain."

Marie heads downstairs thinking pleasant sleep will be a welcome relief. Not yet familiar with the layout of the boat, she takes a wrong turn and sees the words "Captain's Quarters" on one of the doors.

"That's odd," she thinks reading the words underneath. "*Tirips Enivid*. I wonder if it's Latin or something. I must remember to ask him in the morning."

Marie turns around and finds her own sleeping quarters. She enters, prepares herself for bed and slips between the soft cotton sheets. She falls into a deep sleep the moment her head greets the feather pillow. But pleasant dreams do not visit her. Instead, she sees herself caught in a terrible storm in a small dinghy, being tossed around on a violent sea.

A mixture of judgmental family voices howls in the blowing wind. "Who do you think you are, abandoning your daughter and leaving your husband to go on this *pleasure* trip?"

"You are selfish. You should work out your marriage with Lloyd."

"You never think about anybody but yourself. You never appreciated your life, always wanting more."

The whirling voices transform into a whirlpool in the middle of the sea, trapping her small boat. Through the hard driving rain, she can barely see another dinghy from which her daughter Elizabeth, is calling out, "Mommy, Mommy help me!"

Around and around they go. The angry storm pulls both boats deeper into the whirlpool, sucking them down into a vortex. Marie reaches out, trying to grab Elizabeth's outstretched arms. But her daughter moves farther and farther away.

The winds let out one last howl as the boats begin to sink and go underwater. This time she hears Lloyd's voice, "See? You're losing everything that's important to you."

Marie lets out a scream as the water crashes over the boat dragging it down under the water. She wakes up gasping for air. Looking at the clock she realizes she only slept a few hours.

Meanwhile, Barb hears Marie's screams. She runs down the hall, knocks and enters the room. She sits next to Marie and puts an arm around her shoulder to comfort her.

Through her tears, Marie says, "I'm so tired of feeling conflicted. No matter how hard I try to please everyone and do what's expected of me, it's never enough."

"Barb, you know I made a promise not to let Elizabeth grow up around people who don't respect and appreciate her. I support her and nurture the talents God gave her. The expectations of keeping my promise dwindled when I saw how Lloyd treated her over her big achievement. His arrogant attitude caused her a lot of unnecessary pain."

Remembering the hurt in her daughter's eyes causes Marie to start sobbing again. Marie attempts to pull herself together while Barb continues to comfort her saying, "Go ahead Marie, let it out."

"Here I am on this beautiful boat, on a wonderful trip. Why do I wallow around in this pity party instead of enjoying myself? I have no right to feel this way," she says while her sobbing begins to subside.

"Nonsense," says the Captain, now standing in the doorway.

"I'm so sorry," Marie says feeling embarrassed.

"Never apologize for the way you feel," he responds.

"But, I'm ruining your trip," she says with tears streaming down her cheeks.

Captain T shakes his head and silently leaves the doorway. A worried look appears on Marie's face when she sees him leave.

"Oh, Barb now I did it, he's really mad at me."

"No, he's not. Trust me, he's not mad," she says releasing Marie from her arms.

With those words, the Captain reappears at her doorway. "May I come in?"

"Of course, Captain," Marie replies.

He walks to Marie and hands her a small unfinished wooden chest. "For me?" she asks.

"Yes," he says. Marie takes the chest from his hands and thanks him. She runs her hand over the smooth rounded ridge top and pulls up the decorative latch to explore the inside.

The Captain sits next to Marie while she opens the chest. She sees a tiny scroll sitting at the bottom and notices a bronze plate on the inside of the lid. She reads the words engraved on the plate aloud.

"You are the perfection of God's creation and the creation of God's perfection. That makes you a worthy person. God divinely created you to be successful in all things."

Before she can make another sound, the Captain begins to speak. "Marie, God created you from love, making you His child worthy of love. You come into this world with self-worth and no one can take it from you. Nor can you lose it.

"But, you *can* lose sight of it and you *can* forget you are a unique, priceless individual.

"No one can really take your excellence away from you unless you *let them*. It's always there, but at times you may not see it, feel it or acknowledge it. It could be hidden under layers of false beliefs and false messages, buried under years of negativity.

"Marie, think of your self-worth like a buried treasure chest. The treasure chest is worth something… even when empty, battered and weather worn, because it exists.

"Let's take it a step further… Suppose somebody dismantles the treasure chest into smaller pieces. The pieces of wood retain worth because they exist. Those smaller pieces of wood may represent your pain, hurt, your inner beauty and your uniqueness.

"Feelings of unworthiness and inferiority get their beginnings early in life. They take root during the time your brain receives crucial and permanent impressions. Through negative thoughts, false programming, a well-meaning person, a teacher's remark, these are ways you begin to form the belief system about yourself.

"It is important and critical to recognize your innate worth. Your ultimate happiness and sense of well-being virtually depend upon it. When you recognize your true self, you'll strive to fulfill your potential."

"Thank you so much, Captain, this means so much to me," she says pulling the chest close to her heart.

Engrossed in the Captain's story, Marie doesn't notice when Barb leaves the room until she returns with a treasure chest of her own. Marie notices Barb's is filled with gems, pearls, silver and gold.

"My father gave me this when I was a little girl and he taught me how to use the contents to live the life of my dreams."

The Captain assures Marie her chest also contains gems, pearls and silver, but she just can't see them now. "You will begin to see your true treasure when you start to accept yourself as worthy person."

Marie opens her chest again, picks up the scroll and unties the ribbon around it.

At the top, she sees three affirmations. The Captain tells her these affirmations will help her begin the first steps to connecting to her true self again. He instructs her to recite them first thing in the morning when she wakes up and do the same before going to sleep each night.

"Tonight, put the chest on your nightstand. Look at it while you drift off to sleep, repeat this message so it's the last thought in your mind: I choose to see my worthiness because I exist as a child of God."

"Will do, Captain," Marie says with a smile. He returns the smile and she notices a kindness in his gentle loving eyes. His presence makes her feel loved.

Barb and her father hug Marie goodnight and retire to their rooms for the rest of the evening.

CHAPTER 3

Step 1 - All Journeys Start with Hope

Marie falls back to sleep repeating the words: "I choose to see my worthiness because I exist as a child of God."

She sleeps peacefully for the rest of the night and follows the Captain's instructions when she awakens. She removes the scroll from the treasure chest, unrolls it and recites the three affirmations developed to help her recognize her self-worth.

- I am good enough
- I love being me
- I am worth loving

She places the scroll back in the treasure chest and puts it on her nightstand. Then Marie showers, dresses and joins Barb and her father on the deck where they are enjoying breakfast.

"I didn't want to wake you," Barb says. "I figured after last night, you could use the extra sleep." Then she asks, "How are you feeling?"

"Much better, thank you. I noticed it felt uncomfortable doing the affirmations this morning. I hear my mind saying, 'yeah right' when I recite them, not fully believing it."

The Captain replies, "You'll naturally hear back-talk for a while. The strong resistance is your inner self letting you know an area requires extra attention."

"Extra attention?"

"Yes, hearing positive statements about yourself conflicts with your current self-beliefs. It took years of repetition to form your current belief system. Fortunately, it won't take years to replace self-limiting thoughts. Keep repeating them and eventually your new belief system, will start feeling completely natural to you.

"Try this tip when you feel the most resistance. Simply add one of the following phrases, 'I choose', 'I am ready' or 'I decide' in front of the affirmation. Then notice which one gives you the most inner back-talk," the Captain instructs.

"I am worth loving," Marie says, her voice breaking.

"Instead say it this way, 'I decide I am worth loving.' Go ahead and try it," the Captain suggest.

"I decide I am worth loving." Marie notices a slight shift in her resistance. Her inner thoughts didn't argue back with her.

"It did feel different," she says excitingly.

"Here is another trick you can use to boost your results. Add the words *'to believe'* after any of those three phrases. Like *'I choose to believe', 'I am ready to believe', 'I decide to believe'*," the Captain adds.

Marie repeats the affirmation adding *'to believe'* to it. "I decide to believe I am worth loving. That feels even more powerful," she remarks.

The Captain replies, "Keep repeating them and change any with one of those start phrases. Soon you will sense them becoming a part of you."

"I hope so, I want to believe they are true," she states.

"They are," Barb and her farther reply in unison. "The crew set up a buffet in the kitchen. Grab some breakfast and join us here," Barb adds. "It's a gorgeous spread. They prepared scrambled eggs, bacon, French toast, sliced ham and fresh fruit."

Returning to the table with a full plate, Marie pours herself a mug of coffee. She looks down at her breakfast and then at Barb and the Captain with a perplexed look on her face.

"What's wrong, Marie? You look puzzled," Barb asks.

"I am… about everything. Inviting me to come with you, the gift of the treasure chest. Were you *planning* all along for me to come on this trip?"

A large grin takes over the Captain's face and Barb's smile stretches from ear to ear.

"Barb and I have a proposal for you," the Captain confesses.

"A proposal?" Marie asks.

"How would you like to finally unlock the life you deserve, while keeping the promise you made to your daughter?" the Captain asks.

"What do you mean?" Marie replies with surprise. Before she can say anything further, the Captain continues. "How would you like to take a detour to sail through the Ocean of Possibilities and uncover *hidden treasures*, buried deep under years of hurt and pain?

"If you accept and complete the journey, you can follow your heart's desire, live life *your* way, and go far beyond your dreams to create a new legacy for you and your daughter."

He also warns her, "You should know this journey will not be easy. You will face several storms caused by all the emotional abuse you've experienced in your life. You'll battle pirates who will want to steal your dreams. Barb and I will be with you every step of the way on this magical journey, but the decision rests in your hands."

The offer catches Marie completely off guard.

"What about your trip to the Bahamas? Barb, I don't want to interfere with the yearly trip you take with your father. I feel guilty about how I'm ruining this trip already."

Barb replies, "No need to feel guilty, Marie. I told my father about the recent events in your life. It was *his idea* to turn around and include you. He's a great mind-reader."

"The decision still rests with you. Either way we'll enjoy the trip," the Captain adds. "But you don't need to answer yet. Enjoy your breakfast. We'll be near Freeport soon and we can enjoy some island time. When we return to the boat, we'll either continue toward the Bahamas or plot a new course."

After a day of visiting the island and enjoying the sights, as they return to the yacht, Marie announces she's made her decision. "Let's go to the Ocean of Possibilities!"

"You know the trip isn't going to be like today, filled with all fun and sightseeing. There will be times you'll be *tested*. Are you sure?" the Captain asks.

"Yes, I understand and I still want to go," Marie remarks.

The Captain's face breaks into an ear-to-ear grin. "It's my favorite place to sail. You never know exactly what you'll encounter…it's such a thrilling adventure."

Once aboard, he pulls out an old parchment map. "There are many islands and places to see… Ah, but which ones… the choice is yours, Marie. This is *your* adventure. *Your* journey."

Marie replies, "I'm confused. You say the Ocean of Possibilities contains many islands, but I only see one on the map."

The Captain chuckles and puts his finger next to the island on the map. "The journey starts on this island, the Island of Hope, which is the gateway to the Ocean of Possibilities. Get a good night's sleep. It will be a busy day tomorrow. Marie, before you go to sleep, I would like you do something."

"Sure," she replies.

"When you take the scroll out of your treasure chest, hold it against your heart, close your eyes and repeat your affirmations."

"Will do, Captain." She says goodnight, heads down to her room and follows his instructions for her evening affirmation ritual. She falls asleep repeating the words, *"I choose to see my worthiness because I exist as a child of God."*

She falls asleep feeling hopeful for the first time in a long time, sure she's charting a new course for her future. Marie wakes up the next morning feeling energized.

The Magical Essence arrives at the next island and begins docking while Marie readies for the day. She joins Barb on the deck with a lightness in her steps. She feels like a kid again.

As the yacht finishes docking, Marie looks up at the gulls circling above, welcoming them. "Is this the Island of Hope?" Marie inquires.

Captain T comes up behind the girls and answers with a yes.

Marie notices a woman waving while coming toward them as they disembark. Barb and her father wave back.

"Who is she?" Marie asks.

"That's Regina, one of several mentors you will meet on this journey. She will help you see your inner treasure, enabling you to step into the person you were always meant to be."

Dressed smartly in a bright coral and white print blouse and solid coral skirt that flows around her ankles. The rhinestone straps of Regina's sandals reflect the morning sun rays, highlighting the sparkle of her hazel eyes.

The Captain and Barb rush ahead to greet Regina and each give her a warm hug. Marie soon catches up with them.

"Who might this be?" Regina asks with a friendly confident smile.

"Marie, I'd like to introduce you to a very wise woman, Regina," Barb says.

Regina chuckles and extends her hand to Marie's, "Pleasure to meet you."

"Pleasure to meet you, too" Marie says while shaking Regina's hand.

"I'm looking forward to your famous shrimp and grits for breakfast," says a famished Barb. "Marie, they are to die for. Wait until you taste them."

The group walks toward the small town. The morning breeze joins them on their brief walk, releasing the fragrance of tropical flowers along the way. They head toward Hope Island Grille.

Regina opens the door and says to Marie, "Welcome to my place."

Barb and her father take a table near the entrance while Regina invites Marie to join her in the booth overlooking the bay.

"What a beautiful island," Marie remarks looking out the window.

"I agree with you. I love living here. A big difference from the New England town where I use to live. So, Marie, what brings you here today?"

Marie begins to share her reasons for embarking on this journey, finishing with: "Regina, I feel overwhelmed and excited at the same time. It all seems like a dream. I keep expecting to wake up any minute."

The waitress sets down the bowls of shrimp and grits. Marie takes a spoonful into her mouth and remarks, "Absolute heaven. Regina this is *so* good."

"Thank you, Marie. It's a family recipe passed down for generations. When I was a little girl, I use to play 'restaurant' with the neighborhood kids and I would serve my mom's grits."

"So, did you open this restaurant as soon as you were old enough?"

"Not exactly, Marie. My parents didn't think starting a restaurant was a good idea. No security, no future they said. They insisted I go to college, obtain a skill and retire with a pension. I took a secretarial job in the medical field and eventually became an executive director for a major hospital.

"My passion for cooking never went away. I think my husband, Sam, secretly married me for my culinary skills. When I got home from work, my kitchen was my place to release stress. Seeing my husband and children enjoy the meals I created gave me such pleasure.

"Sam encouraged me to start a restaurant when I retired, but I thought it was too late. Five years ago, he passed away. My children are grown and pursuing their own lives. I felt lost and regretted not listening to my husband. I met the Captain and he helped me believe in myself. He made me realize it's *never* too late.

"I realized when you keep a glimmer of hope alive, anything is possible. So, I am curious, Marie, what deep passion resides inside of you?"

Marie shares with Regina her childhood dream of wanting to become a famous jewelry designer. The more she talks about it the more excited she gets. Regina hears the passion in her new friend's voice.

"Marie, hope is wonderful, but useless without action… hope without action is just a wish. Do you really want to make your dream happen? Are you ready to take action?"

"Yes, I am!" Marie says enthusiastically.

"Good. Let's take the next step."

Regina stands up and invites Marie to take her hand while they walk to the side door. "Let me show you what must be done next."

Marie looks at Barb and her father chatting companionably while enjoying their breakfast. She doesn't want to disturb them. Captain T looks up as Regina and Marie get ready to leave.

"Captain, I do believe this young lady is passionate about her dream and keeping her promise. She wants to take the next step on this journey," Regina states.

"Marie, remember how I told you the journey to the Ocean of Possibilities begins on this island?" the Captain adds.

"Yes, Captain, I remember," Marie answers.

"The decision always rests in your hands. Only you can choose to continue. This is the first of several trials to test your commitment to changing your life. Are you sure you want to do this?"

Nervously, Marie replies, "Yes."

Regina reaches her right hand into a jar by the door and pulls out a small object. She places it in her left palm, closing her hand around it to hide it from.

"Ready to go?" asks Regina, holding her right hand out to Marie again, inviting her to take it.

"Go where?" she inquires.

The Captain replies, "Regina will take you to the other side of this island to Harbor Blame. It's through this harbor one enters the Ocean of Possibilities. Barb and I will see you when you complete this first step."

Barb gives Maria a hug, and whispers, "Trust Regina and believe you're worthy of your dreams. I'll see you shortly."

Marie takes Regina's hand, and they walk out the door taking the stone path toward Harbor Blame.

CHAPTER 4

Seduction at Harbor Blame

The stone path soon turns sandy, winding its way through a small grove of coconuts. Honeysuckle plants dot the edge of the pathway.

"This is a small island," Regina states. "We'll be on the other side in about 30 minutes. I prefer a slow, leisurely pace. What about you, Marie?"

"I do too. I love the smell of honeysuckle," Marie says dreamily.

"The Ocean of Possibilities lies through the small strait of Harbor Blame. Unfortunately, many let the hope of their dreams die there." Regina comments sadly.

"Why does hope die there?" Marie asks.

"Legend goes the harbor is named after the man who settled there, Gabriel Blame. Gabriel's father, Charles, started out with nothing, went to college, became a lawyer and created one of the largest law firms on the mainland."

Regina continues, "Gabriel and his eldest brother, Fredrick, grew up with the benefits of wealth their father created and he loved indulging the whims of his sons. He wanted the best for them, enabling them to follow his path into the firm.

"Fred epitomized the role of the model child, according to his father and societal expectations. He excelled at his goals. Some of his accomplishments include playing basketball, becoming a track star, senior-year class president, a member of the National Honor Society and leading his debate team to the State Championship. Charles proudly bragged about his son's achievements to anybody who would listen. Naturally, Fred went to a prestigious Ivy League school and then followed in his father's footsteps into the law firm.

His second son, the very handsome Gabriel, relied instead on his own wit and charisma."

Regina continues, "Gabriel loved acting and his teachers remarked about his exceptional gift. He shined on stage, especially in front of a live audience. Performing offered him a welcome relief from the many expectations laid upon him because of his brother's success.

"At first, Gabriel tried to pursue a career in law to please his father. But he didn't apply himself and flunked out after the first quarter. Going against his father's wishes, he went to California to pursue his dream of acting, a frivolous goal according to his father.

"Gabriel arrived in Los Angles, no longer the high school drama star, and found himself unprepared to handle the fierce competition. He expected his father to cover all his expenses while waiting for his big break. He figured his father owed him for forcing him to attend college in the first place. After all, he paid for Fredrick's education and supported him until he joined the firm.

His father told him if he would go back to college, he would help him financially but he was on his own if continued to pursue this reckless acting path."

Regina adds, "Gabriel felt it beneath him to take low-paying odd jobs like his fellow actors waiting for acting roles. One of Gabriel's new California friends, told him he could make quick and easy cash selling drugs. Soon he gave up on acting, was arrested and went to jail. He blamed his father for his failures."

Regina continues, "He blamed the judge for imprisoning him. In jail, he heard about an island that led to a place where dreams can happen. Inmates told him he could start a new life there. Upon release, he came straight here to the Island of Hope."

Regina and Marie pause at the top of a small hill. Looking down, they see a sprawling harbor town with a misty covered harbor.

Regina continues the story while they walk down the small hill into town. She points to the water and says, "The only way to sail through the Ocean of Possibilities is to pass through the strait to the Island of Responsibility. From there, you can sail anywhere you want.

"Think about this and apply it to your current circumstances: Gabriel refused to take responsibility for his life. He let bitterness, anger, jealousy and resentment *consume* him. He blamed everyone including his father, brother, the drama teacher, and his lawyers, for the way his life turned out.

"He never accepted any fault for his mistakes, decisions and actions. He felt the world *owed him* because of the tyrannical father he was made to endure. To this day, Gabriel still lives on this side of the island, telling his story repeatedly. He can't get past it.

"Unfortunately, many people find it easier to blame others instead of *taking action* to change their lives. Hope dies because they don't take responsibility. They give up and spend their rest of their miserable lives *harboring blame*."

When they reach town, Regina unfolds her hand, revealing the shell she took from the jar in the restaurant. She places it in Marie's hand. Marie looks down at the shell resting in her palm.

"This shell represents hope. Hope is knowing something better will happen for you despite life's disappointments and setbacks. It keeps you connected to the Divine, the source of everything possible. By holding hold onto hope, you will more likely make it. You hold your future *in your hands*."

They reach the shore and walk toward the pier. Marie notices a set of steps descending onto a wooden platform resting in the harbor. Tied to the platform is a small row boat.

Regina comments, "Looks like I need to find your escort."

"My escort?" Marie inquires.

"Yes," Regina says pointing to the rowboat. "The man who will row you out of the harbor. Sit on this bench and rest. I'll be back shortly with Paul. I think I know where I can find him. But first Marie, a word of warning. Gabriel is quite handsome and irresistibly charming. He chose to give up on his dreams and wasted his talents. He will try to talk you into giving up on yours. His words will sound very seductive."

Several women walking along the shore notice Regina leaving to find Paul. "There goes that woman again, peddling her 'happiness and hope crap'," one says loudly enough for Marie to hear.

The group stops in front of Marie without acknowledging her presence as they continue their conversation. "What does she know? She and that captain character promising people can live their dreams. What a bunch of bull."

"They fill people with hope and expect them to do the impossible," another chimes in.

"If someone handed everything to me, I'd be all happy and successful too. Some people are born lucky," says another.

Marie notices another irritated-looking lady joining the group. "That 'hope lady' doesn't get it. My parents abused me and constantly put me down. My life would be totally different if my parents loved me for *me*. No such luck. I can't change the past, now can I?

The words *"My life would be totally different if my parents loved me for me"* sent a jolt like a lightning rod through Marie. How many times did she think the same thought? Looking up, she notices a very handsome, impeccably dressed man joining the group.

"Ladies, ladies, you will give our guest the wrong impression of our wonderful town," he says looking at Marie and smiling.

This gorgeous man walks toward her causes her heart to skip a beat. She notices his dark, mid-length hair blowing freely in the breeze. His Spanish style beard accentuates his distinctive high cheekbones, giving him a "debonair" appearance.

Gabriel Blame takes her hand, brings it to his lips, gently kisses it and introduces himself. "My name is Gabriel. Who is this beautiful, enchanting creature before me?" he asks.

"Marie," she responds dreamily.

"What brings you to our fair town today?" he asks sitting next to her, still holding her hand. His dark, sensual eyes gazing deeply into hers.

"I'm waiting for someone to take me to the Ocean of Possibilities."

As the wind blew a fine mist from the sea to the shoreline, Marie looks out over the harbor. She begins to feel nervous about traveling in the deteriorating weather conditions.

"Someone told me this was the only way to the Ocean of Possibilities." Marie says with a questioning tone in her voice.

With the diminishing weather conditions, Marie wonders if there is another way to reach the Ocean of Possibilities. She thinks to herself, *"Perhaps, my past upbringing will spare her from going through harbor."*

Marie looks at Gabriel and says, "Can I ask you a question?"

"Yes, Marie, please ask." he answers.

"I just heard someone say they experienced abuse from their parents. They pointed out how life would be different if only they grew up with unconditional love. Shouldn't I hold my parents and teachers responsible for my misery too?" she asks Gabriel.

"Of course," he replies. "By parental default, they acquired complete power and control over you. How could you question them at your young age when your survival depended on them?" he says reassuring her.

"Your upbringing, experiences and circumstances led to the life you live now. If you didn't grow up in a nurturing environment, you were probably robbed of your potential," he continued.

"Oh my gosh!" Marie exclaims. Her eyes widen upon this revelation. "It's like my parents never accepted me. Trying to make me into something I'm not!"

"I know how you feel. My father always compared me to my perfect older brother. If I had a dollar for every time he said, 'why can't you be more like him?' I'd be rich," Gabriel says empathetically.

"Mine too. And so, did my teachers, 'Why can't you be more like your older sister?'" Marie says, finally feeling validated *Finally!* she thought, *somebody who understands me.*

"You received a bad hand in life through no fault of your own. Betrayed by the very people who said they loved you." Gabriel said in a sympathetic voice.

"Yes," Marie agrees angrily.

"Let me guess," he started. "I bet Regina told you to move forward with your life, *you* must accept responsibility for something you weren't in control of in the first place."

"Yes," Marie replies with more anger in her voice, feeling betrayed by those who said they care about her.

"Does that sound fair to you?" Gabriel remarks, enticing Marie to agree with him.

"No, it doesn't," Marie agrees. "It doesn't sound fair at all."

The wind continues to blow harder and she hears the waves crashing around the rocks tossing the small rowboat. Fear grows larger her heart.

Fog begins to blanket the town and Marie barely notices Regina returning with a man dressed in a bright red polo shirt and khaki pants.

"Marie, meet Paul," Regina states. "We call him the Professor. He will row you out of the harbor."

Before Paul could respond to the introduction, an annoyed Marie points to the choppy water tossing the small boat about and says, "In that? You want me to risk my life in these treacherous waters? It's ridiculous," Marie shouts at Regina.

"And now you want me to take responsibility for the results caused by my parents and teachers words and actions? The way they treated me put my life on this path," Marie says trembling with anger and disbelief.

Marie moves closer to the group of women. She looks over at Gabriel smiling at her, nodding in agreement.

"I just met you. I don't know you. Why should I trust you?" Marie asks Regina.

The words uttered by Regina, took her by surprise. "Marie, you're right to ask why you should trust me. Let me ask you a question, do you trust your best friend, Barb?"

"Of course. Barb's never given me a reason not to trust her. I decided to go on this journey of that trust."

"You can choose right *now* to take this opportunity to live the life you desire. I know it's easier to blame others instead of taking responsibility for your future. It's scary to leave behind what you know, and feels comfortable to you," Regina says.

Still doubting Regina, Marie lets go of the shell she is holding in her hand. Surprisingly, it makes a loud echo with a tinkling sound when it meets the ground. Marie wonders how she could hear it dropping onto the sand. For the first time, she looks down to the shore and notices that it is covered in layers and layers of shells. Most of them *crushed*.

She remembers Regina saying this is the place where hope dies. She heard the Captain's voice whispering in the wind, "It's time to fulfill your promise to your daughter. Create a new legacy for Elizabeth and future generations. It's time to stop harboring blame."

She picks up the shell she just dropped, realizing only *she* is responsible for her future, her life and only *she* can change it. She looks at it in the palm of her hand, holds tighter, as if, holding on to hope, and looks over to Regina saying, "I do trust you and Barb."

After taking a deep breath, Marie exhales and on her next inhale breathes in the resolve to continue to hold on to hope for her future. Confidently she states, "I'm ready to step into the rowboat. How else will I ever experience the Ocean of Possibilities?"

CHAPTER 5

Step 2 - The Strait of Lost Dreams

Gabriel shakes his head, looking frustrated as he realizes he's lost Marie. He joins the group of women on the bench and a worried expression creases his brow. He watches the other women closely fearing they too might wake up and follow Marie to the boat.

Paul introduces himself, extending his hand to Marie. She shakes his hand saying, "Hi Paul, I'm Marie."

"I know the harbor looks scary," he says looking down the dock at the choppy waters. "I've navigated many folks through worse than this. I promise I can safely maneuver us through the harbor and out through the Strait of Lost Dreams," he says in a reassuring voice.

"Lost Dreams?" Marie asks as they walk down the pier to the platform.

"Yes, Marie. Those who don't take responsibility for their future, and continue to blame others for their situation, are holding onto their past. They choose to abandon hope, leave their dreams behind, and set up permanent lodging harboring blame."

When they reach the stairs, Regina turns to Marie and says, "I confidently turn you over to Paul's capable hands."

Regina points to the shell in Marie's palm and tells her, "The shell's journey to reach this island started a thousand miles away. Yet it arrived here on shore intact, despite the tossing and turning by the stormy seas.

"Let this shell remind you that even the tiniest and most-fragile objects can survive the storms of life. *You can too.*"

Marie whispers, "Thank you." Regina hugs her and whispers in her ear, "I believe in you."

Looking down at the choppy waters, an expression of worry comes over Marie and her fear causes her to shake. Paul notices the hesitation on Marie's face and extends a hand. She takes as he helps her down the steps and assists her into the rowboat. He puts the oars in the water and starts rowing toward the Strait of Lost Dreams.

The waves throw them both off balance. Marie quickly puts on her life vest and holds on tight. Paul gives a reassuring smile which briefly calms her for a moment.

Through the fog, Marie catches a glimpse of many towering, rocky formations in the harbor. The sight of them causes an uneasy feeling in the pit of her stomach. Without realizing it, she begins speaking her thoughts aloud.

"This is nuts," she mumbles. "Maybe Gabriel was right. Is this worth risking my life? I really didn't have it so bad."

Paul stops rowing. "We can always turn around," he replies.

"What?" a surprised Marie responds, not realizing she was talking loud enough to be heard.

"We don't need to go any further," he says. "I can't *force* you to go. This decision, your future, rests in *your* hands. I'm going to tell you something that will be hard to hear. I know you're hurting inside. You are right. You deserved unconditional love.

"Your past doesn't define who you truly you are. And you can't move forward holding onto the blame. It's time to decide. It doesn't matter if you lived an unhappy, lousy childhood or an awesome one, the responsibility for realizing your future goals and dreams falls on *your* shoulders now.

"It might seem easier blaming others and staying stuck rather than accepting personal responsibility. Whoever or whatever you place blame on, you give your personal power and control over to them."

Marie ponders Paul's words.

He continues, "Blaming is a means of control by looking outside yourself for the center of power. The sooner you stop looking outside yourself, the sooner you can do something about your future.

"Everything you need to succeed, to experience the life you desire, you'll find *inside* of you. It's your inner treasure. So, before we can continue, assure me you want to take the next step in your journey and sail the Ocean of Possibilities."

Marie sighs, takes a deep breath, and exhales. She recalls the words Captain T told her on the first night, *'If you accept and complete the journey, you can follow your heart's desire, live life your way, and go beyond your dreams. You will fulfill the promise for your daughter and create a new legacy for her and future generations.'*

Marie gulps and says, "Row."

Paul rows closer to the craggy towers and maneuvers around them. Suddenly, Marie notices they are not rock formations at all, but a heaping pile of discarded *treasure chests*, just like the one the Captain gave her.

"Oh my gosh!!!" Marie says alarmingly.

Paul replies. "These treasure chests represent the discarded hopes and dreams of people who decided not to see their self-worth. They couldn't grasp how fulfilling their dreams could make a difference in the world."

"Now I see why they call this the Strait of Lost Dreams," Marie says sadly. She realizes how close she came to discarding her own hopes and goals.

As they pass through the Strait, the waters calm and the fog turns to a light mist. The sun battles to break through until it finally triumphs. The narrow Strait opens onto beautiful, clear turquoise water.

"Welcome to the Ocean of Possibilities, the voyage everyone is meant to take. You probably realize by now not everybody makes it this far," Paul says.

"I made it. I'm really here!" she says excitingly. "It looks like paradise."

As the clouds part, Marie's gaze focuses on a small island with gorgeous white glistening sand. A beautiful pink granite resort sparkles in the sun. Paul promptly drops the outboard motor into the ocean and navigates toward the island.

The nearer they come to shore, the better Marie feels, glad she came this far.

She notices the figures of two people waiting on the shore and recognizes Barb and her father. Then she glances back at the Strait of Lost Dreams, but the glare from the sun makes it impossible to see. She thought, *"It's almost like you would never know it existed."*

She breathes a sigh of relief, knowing she made the right decision.

Paul stops the motor and pulls it in to keep it from getting stuck in the approaching shore. Putting oars in the water, he rows close enough to throw a rope, the Captain catches it and pulls the boat in.

Marie can't wait. She leaps out of the boat, jumping into the waves and running through the knee-deep waters toward Barb. They embrace like long lost friends.

"I'm so happy you chose to continue this journey," Barb exclaims.

"Me too," Marie answers. The four of them walk along the beach toward the house. Marie looks back and sees the Magical Essence anchored in the ocean. She spots a blue dinghy resting on the shore.

"Well, at least the ride back to the boat will prove less challenging," she says pointing to the dinghy.

Everyone chuckles and Paul says, "Welcome, Marie, to the Island of Responsibility. You just completed the first two steps toward the life you richly deserve."

"First *two* steps?" Marie inquires.

"Yes," says Captain T. "The first is hope. Hope for a different, better life where your dreams *can* come true. Hope for the positive outcomes you want in your life.

The second is taking responsibility for your life, your actions, and your thoughts now and into the future."

Paul adds, "Marie, everyone's journey across the Ocean of Possibilities starts with these two steps. Where you go from here will be up to you."

He continues, "You will chart your course toward your destiny, but before we begin, I'm hungry. Getting someone through that strait always works up my appetite. Let's enjoy an early supper. I'm sure my cook, Louise, prepared something wonderful."

Marie looks at Paul and says, "Since we met, I can't stop thinking how familiar you look to me. I bet where we met before will come to me over supper. I'm too famished to think right now."

"Come with me, Marie. "Let me show you to your room. Don't you love this grand resort? I always look forward to staying here," says Barb.

Marie follows Barb to her room and notices her treasure chest sitting on the night stand. "My chest!" Marie exclaims ecstatically.

"I hope you don't mind. I also took the liberty of bringing some clothes and toiletries. If I missed anything, we can take the dinghy out to the boat and grab it," Barb suggest.

"I don't mind. It looks like you got everything I will need for tonight." Marie walks over to the chest, opens it and places the shell into it.

"You look exhausted. Would you like to rest before suppertime?" a smiling Barb asks.

"Yes, I would. Thanks, Barb. Thank you for being a good friend," Marie replies.

Marie lies down on the bed and slowly drifts off when suddenly she remembers why Paul looks familiar.

Last year, Barb gave her a book entitled, *"Personal Empowerment: The Secret to Living Your Dreams,"* written by Paul DiSalvaro. His photograph on the back cover didn't sport the scholarly glasses he wore today.

She remembers his philosophy hitting her like a lightning bolt. He wrote about the importance of keeping self-made promises in relationship to achieving your goals. Soon exhaustion takes over and Marie drifts off to sleep.

A knock on the door awakens Marie. She looks at the clock and notices it's an hour later.

"Come in," she says.

Barb opens the door and lets Marie know supper is ready. They join Paul and the Captain already sitting at the table on the outdoor patio. Paul stands up to lend a hand to a brunette woman carrying a tray of ice tea and glasses.

"Marie, meet my wife, Shirley," Paul says taking the tray from her hands and placing it on the table.

Standing up, Marie takes Shirley's hand and says, "Pleasure to meet you."

Shirley responds, "My pleasure too. You experienced quite an adventure today, didn't you, Marie?"

"Yes, I did. I also remember why Paul looks familiar," Marie responds.

"I read your book and I must admit it made me realize I was breaking a promise I made to myself and God. I knew right then and there that I would need to make some important decisions and difficult changes, if I wanted different life."

"Ah, Marie, you took a step toward taking responsibility for your life. You didn't even consciously know it, did you?" Paul asks.

Supper arrives before she can answer the question.

"Marie, let me introduce you to Louise, the head chef for this resort." Paul says with a big smile on his face. "Our guests love her infamous crab cakes. They are a crowd favorite."

Louise sets down a plate in front of Marie. "Nice to meet you, Louise. Thank you. They look delicious. Can't wait to try them."

"Enjoy," Louise says.

Paul pours Chardonnay into the chilled wine glasses. He raises his glass to propose a toast. "To old friends and new friendships. The most valuable gems in anyone's life."

"Cheers," everyone responds while clinking their glasses together.

"It's gorgeous here. What a beautiful place," Marie says soaking in the beauty. She continues the conversation with a question. "Paul, you said the crab cakes were a favorite with the guests. Will other guests join us tonight? I don't remember seeing anybody else here."

Paul starts, "Marie, most of the time you will find this place filled with up-and-coming authors. The limited distractions on The Island of Responsibilities make it the perfect place to write. Many find the beauty of this small island inspiring and the perfect place to pursue their dreams of writing the next great novel.

"It's just us right now and a few of the staff. The solitude allows me to explore the writing projects floating around in my brain. These peaceful and uplifting surroundings will help me create my next best-selling book."

"Paul, I want to apologize for my behavior earlier. I got confused and scared because I let Gabriel get to me," Marie states.

"Yes, you became quite vocal just before we entered the Strait, Marie. No apology necessary, though. You made the critical choice to let go of blame and self-pity to rise above your circumstances. Often people choose to hold onto it their entire lives, then wonder why they find themselves in constant pain."

Marie asks, "I feel a little confused. Yes, I understand how taking personal responsibility for my future lets me move forward. However, how can I totally let go of the beliefs my parents and teachers taught me?"

Captain T answers Marie's question, "Choosing personal responsibility means accepting accountability for something within your power. This gives you the freedom to exercise the ability and authority to decide to choose and act on your own. You alone are answerable for your actions. Taking responsibility for all facets of your life gives you the power to move forward in a more positive way, despite the challenges you encountered in the past or may encounter in the future."

Paul takes over the conversation. "When you take responsibility for your actions, instead of playing the victim or blaming outside forces, you give yourself the power to *change*. The power of personal responsibility allows you to grow into your potential."

"I think I'm beginning to understand," says Marie on a positive note. "Now I can choose to keep the negative programming from the past and let it hold me back or reject it and replace it with positive beliefs."

"It's a chance for you to rewrite your story, From Victim to Victor," Paul states.

The Captain adds, "I told you to expect to encounter difficulties and trials on this journey. You will meet other wise individuals who will teach you to purge, heal and cleanse yourself of the past, pains, labels and beliefs holding back from your potential.

When you stepped into the rowboat it was a step into your own personal power."

Paul says to Marie, "Let me share what personal power really means:

"Potential Optimized With Extraordinary Results™""

"Wow! What an impressive acronym, Paul," Marie exclaims. "She turns to the Captain and adds, "Thanks for your reassuring words."

Shirley stands up to clear the empty plates, "Who wants Key Lime Pie?" she asks.

The response is a hardy, "I do!" Paul helps Shirley and they return with pie for everyone.

Marie notices Paul setting down a beautifully-wrapped present the size of a thin notebook.

After dessert, He gives Marie the present and says, "An important aspect of taking responsibility for yourself comes from knowing what you want to achieve in your life.

"Set goals that will help you get there. Then focus your time and efforts on working toward and accomplishing your goals. Take responsibility for your actions, learn from what happens and adjust your plans to continue moving toward your goals. You will create the life you desire."

"Thanks, Paul." Marie says.

Marie unwraps the present, opens the box and under the tissue paper she finds a sea foam green leather bound book. Marie traces her fingers over gold embossed lettering on the cover that reads, "Navigating the Ocean of Possibilities Guidebook."

Paul says, "This guidebook will help you chart your course."

Marie reads the poem on the inside front cover:

> "Watch your thoughts; they become words.
> Watch your words; they become actions.
> Watch your actions; they become habits.
> Watch your habits; they become your character.
> Watch your character; it becomes your destiny.
>
> ~Margaret Thatcher"

The Captain tells Marie, "Controlling your thoughts is within your power. You can choose to accept the ones that support you and let go of those that don't. Open the guidebook to the 'Thoughts' section."

The guidebook contains several blank sections, except for the first, which is imprinted with the words 'Chart Your Course' and the last is called 'Thoughts.' Blank pages fill the rest of the guidebook with a pocket page in the back."

Marie follows The Captain's instructions. She reads the title line on the first page, "Where Are Your Thoughts Taking You?" Followed by: "Identify the thoughts and beliefs no longer serving you."

Captain T continues, "Whenever a negative thought or limiting belief enters your mind, write it here," he says pointing to the page, "Think of it as a limiting belief brain dump."

Marie chuckles and says, "I like this idea. Thanks, Captain."

"Paul, I don't know how to thank you. It's beautiful. The words in the poem give me a lot to think about. They speak volumes about harnessing our true power," Marie says pointing to the inside cover.

"Yes, they truly are powerful, Marie," Paul agrees. "If you take them to heart."

"Something just occurred to me," Marie announces. "Responsibility is like this secret, surprising power source all of us can use to create the life we want."

"Marie, you got it!" remarks Barb, smiling from ear to ear.

"What a perspective, Marie," shouts Paul. "In fact, you just inspired my next book. I now know the title, 'Create the Life You Want Using a Surprising Power Source.' If you don't mind, I will retreat to my study now and write these thoughts down before they escape me."

Everyone offers Paul their good wishes for his writing.

"Speaking of inspiration," the Captain says looking at Marie, "We continue our journey at sunrise and will need to know where to go. Your goals, dreams and desires will guide us through The Ocean of Possibilities.

"First, you need to write out your ideal life. Start by dreaming about where you want to be one year from today. The sun sets in a few hours and the ocean boardwalk gives you a front row seat to watch this breathtaking event. Take your guidebook and let the setting sun inspire your imagination. Write from your heart."

"Yes, Captain," she answers.

Marie takes the guidebook and thanks Shirley for the wonderful meal, then she walks to one of the boardwalk decks. Barb, her father and Shirley remain at the table, continuing to enjoy each other's company.

Marie makes herself comfortable on a lounge chair and begins to write. She goes to the first section of the guidebook, turns the divider and reads the next page with the following instructions:

'Charting Your Course can propel you toward an exciting and abundant life. Let your imagination go and write a vision of your life a year from today with limitless possibilities.

Start with this question: What is your heart's desire?'

Marie is so engrossed in her thoughts she doesn't notice the sun slipping behind the horizon. Only when Barb joins her with two glasses of wine to toast the end of a transforming day, does she realize the amount of time that has passed.

"We will wake up early tomorrow to start our day. I'm going to turn in and get a good night's sleep," Barb informs Marie.

"I'll join you shortly, Barb," Marie says. "I'd like to sit and let my mind unwind."

"On second thought, I could use some unwinding myself," Barb replies.

The two friends sit in silence, listening to the ocean waves and letting the evening envelope them before calling it a night.

Later, Marie enters her room and notices a note placed next to her wooden treasure chest. She opens it and realizes it's from Paul.

"Thanks for the inspiration today. You can now add three more affirmations to your nightly ritual.

- *I rise above all limitations*
- *I have the power to make changes*
- *I create wonderful new beliefs for myself*

See you in the morning.
Love Paul"

Marie is amazed when she realizes she became the inspiration for a best-selling author's new book. *It's so nice to meet people who value my contributions and appreciates me,* she thinks. *A girl could get use to this!*

She takes the scroll and writes the three new affirmations at the bottom of the list. She holds the chest next to her heart, closes her eyes and recites the affirmations.

Marie falls asleep repeating the words she said the previous night, *"I choose to see my worthiness because I exist as a child of God."*

CHAPTER 6

A Special Compass for a Magical Adventure

Marie wakes up, rubs her eyes and looks over at the window of her resort room. She expected to see some signs of daylight around the coverings, but it still looks dark outside.

She opens the blinds, opens the sliding door and walks onto the balcony. *Not totally dark. The horizon looks a little lighter,* she thinks to herself, taking in a deep breath of the cool ocean breeze.

The sun appears anxious to peek over the horizon, announcing its intention with a streak of red and orange resting on the dark blue ocean. Marie reflects on the beginning of a new day and thinks this is a new beginning for her too. Today she starts her journey sailing the Ocean of Possibilities.

A thrilling feeling sweeps over her as she dashes back into the room, quickly changing her clothes and gathering her things. Picking up the treasure chest, she realizes she forgot her morning ritual. She closes her eyes and repeats the six affirmations.

She consciously makes the effort to feel the words, not just repeat them. The words give her the courage to start the next phase of her journey. Smiling, she takes a deep breath.

She catches up with everybody in the lobby and they head toward the shore where the dinghy awaits them. Captain T, Marie and Barb thank Paul and Shirley for a wonderful time.

Paul takes Marie's hand, hugs her and says, "Don't let the sparkle in your eyes dim. You are worthy of your dreams. *I believe in you.*"

"Thank you, Paul," Marie says smiling.

The glistening reflection of the sun on the horizon signals it's time for them to depart. The Captain pushes the dinghy off the shore and rows toward the Magical Essence. When they reach waters deep enough to drop the motor, the Captain pulls up the oar and starts the engine.

With everybody back on board the sailboat, Barb and Pat get comfortable on one of the couches in the main salon.

The Captain walks into the room with an old, antique map.

"Okay, Marie, plot our course!" he says smiling at her while unrolling the parchment on the coffee table in front of them. Marie looks down and only sees two islands, Hope and Responsibility.

"What?!" Marie responds, "I don't know anything about plotting a sailing course."

Captain T reassures her, "You know more than you think. This is the Ocean of Possibilities. You wrote out your vision last night, didn't you?"

"Yes, I did."

"Marie, *your dreams and desires create the map of your life*. Close your eyes and think about the vision you wrote down. Think how it will feel when you achieve it. Feel it from your *heart*. Visualize it. See yourself living it. When you're ready, open your eyes, and rub your hand over the map."

Marie follows the Captain's instructions and five more islands suddenly appear on the map. Marie looks down in amazement.

"This truly is a magical journey," she says in awe.

"Yes, it is, Marie. These are the other islands you will visit. You will meet five more mentors. They will help you embrace your self-worth and uncover your inner greatness."

Marie looks more closely at the map and notices their names: Island of Forgiveness, Island of Gratitude, Island of Faith and Trust and Island of Self-Empowerment.

"Captain," Marie asks, "Which one do we visit next?"

"Marie, *your thoughts will navigate us through these waters*. But first, you'll need an important instrument to make sure we head in the right direction. An item no experienced Captain sails without."

Captain T reaches into his pocket and pulls out a compass. He places the antique in her hand. Marie looks at it and notices the "N" is replaced with the letters "ME."

Looking confused she says, "I don't understand. Doesn't a compass need *north* on it? How is this compass going to make sure we're going in the right direction?"

The Captain smiles at Marie while answering, "This special ocean needs a *special* compass. We all come into the world with everything we need for the happiness and success we're meant to experience.

"Your inner compass, your heart, will let you know if your decisions, actions and thoughts will *take you from or lead you to* your goals and dreams. When you follow your heart, and listen to your inner voice, the compass points to ME. Your true self, your true ME, your Magical Essence. It knows how to sail you to the life of your heart's desires."

"That's the name of your boat!" Marie exclaims.

"No, that's the name of your journey," the Captain replies laughing.

The Captain continues explaining. "The Divine Spirit of the Universe, your Creator, desires only success and happiness for you. He places the dreams within you so you can experience the wonderful life He wants for you."

"Oh, Captain," Marie says hopefully, "I so want to believe those words."

Marie looks down at the parchment map on the table and notices the "North" arrow now appears as the letters ME. *Just like the compass! Pointing to True ME.*

"Sailing the Ocean of Possibilities uses a different compass. One relying on True ME instead of true North for navigation," the Captain comments.

Looking at the compass in her hand and the map below Marie announces, "If I'm reading this correctly, it looks like we visit the Island of Forgiveness next."

Captain T looks over her shoulder and says, "Yes," in agreement.

The chef announces breakfast is ready. Everybody heads toward the dining area. After eating, the Captain says they'll reach the Island of Forgiveness in about three hours.

"Marie, would you like to play some cards?" Barb asks.

"Yes, but if I'm reading the clock correctly, it's a good time for me to call Elizabeth. I sent a text message last night and can't wait to share all the excitement with her." Marie replies.

"Great idea, let's call the girls first."

Marie enters her cabin and notices the crew brought her overnight bag and placed the treasure chest on the night stand. She unpacks the bag, lies on top of the bed and covers herself with the colorful throw from the chair in her room.

She phones Elizabeth. Her daughter sounds excited about camp and Marie feels a sense of relief knowing she and McKenzie are enjoying themselves. Elizabeth loves hearing about her mom's trip and can't wait to talk to her the next day. Marie promises she'll text her after her visit to the Island of Forgiveness. She tells Elizabeth how much she loves her before hanging up.

Congratulations, you found the first item on your treasure hunt. You can retrieve it at www.annrusnak.com/treasure1

CHAPTER 7

Step 3 - Island of Forgiveness

Marie and Barb wrap up their card game when they see the Island of Forgiveness ahead.

"We will use the dinghy to go ashore. Marie, you'll need your guidebook," the Captain announces. They take the steps down to the boarding platform where one of the crew members, Carl, helps them into the small boat.

When they reach the dock, a woman with long wavy brown hair, and wearing a striped caftan, walks toward them She greets everyone with a cheery hello. Marie notices a softness in her eyes that matches the peacefulness in her face.

The Captain introduces Marie to Judith.

"Marie, pleasure to meet you. I would be honored if you would join me for some tea at my cottage," Judith says.

"Don't worry about us," says Barb. "My dad and I need to run an errand. We'll meet you in a bit."

Marie walks with Judith to her cottage where the front is graced with a beautiful flower garden. Judith opens the porch door, removes her sandals and motions for Marie to take a seat.

"I'll return shortly. Just make yourself comfortable," Judith says smiling.

Marie removes her shoes and looks around the invitingly attractive screened-in room. The way the sun cascades through the space, Marie feels like she stepped into a peaceful and loving sanctuary.

Marie sits in one of the white Adirondack chairs and comfortably sinks into the vibrant striped cushion. The furniture compliments the braided rug and an array of palm trees and tropical plants envelope her.

Judith returns carrying a tray with a silver tea and coffee set and a plate of scones and biscotti. Marie lends a hand by setting the tray down on the wicker coffee table. Marie thinks to herself, *What a perfect mid-morning treat.*

"Coffee or tea?" Judith inquires.

"Tea, please," she answers as Judith pours the tea into the water-colored china cup.

Marie looks at the bookstand and notices a wooden treasure chest, similar to Barb's, and brimming with gems, pearls, silver and gold.

"Oh, you own a chest too," Marie says.

"Everybody does. The chest represents an outward reflection of the inner treasure trove of your unique self," Judith replies with a wink.

"The Captain said something similar when he gave me my chest," Marie said agreeing with Judith. "Mine isn't filled yet. I guess this journey will help me with that."

"Yours *is* filled, Marie, you just don't see it right now. Would you, please, bring my treasure chest over to me?"

Marie picks up the chest, sits down and hands it to Judith who removes a single silver coin.

She begins, "Marie, silver is one of the world's most versatile and indispensable metals. The unique combination of characteristics not found in any other single element makes silver so valuable. *Just like you.*

The silver represents self-respect/self-love.

Self-respect builds and shapes the attributes of our values like honesty, confidence and integrity. Possessing a healthy self-respect allows you to accept others' differences and to love yourself so you can love others.

When you respect yourself, it means trusting to say and do only what feels right for you. Honor your inner voice. Keep the promises you make to yourself and others.

Self-love and respect live at the very core of your wellbeing, your joy, your self-empowerment, and your ability to create and enjoy the kind of life you want."

Judith continues, "I'm a big movie buff…love watching them. Have you seen the film *28 Days** featuring Sandra Bullock (as Gwen) and Viggo Mortensen (as Eddie) in a rehab/treatment center? I love this movie, yet my husband *hates* it."

"No, I haven't seen it," Marie replies.

Judith shares, "The reason I love it is because I can relate to it. I stayed in a treatment center myself once.

In the movie, Gwen and Eddie develop a friendship at the rehab center. Part of their treatment requires doing chores around the facility. One day while cleaning out the horse stalls, Eddie starts sharing some of the terrible things he did while addicted to drugs.

He asks Gwen to share some of her stories but she flatly refuses and made excuses that 'drunks don't remember what they do.' The last thing Gwen wanted was to drudge up the last 15 years and humiliate herself in front of this guy.

They argue and Gwen insults Eddie.

Later she seeks him out to apologize. She tells him she didn't want to share because she felt if he really knew what horrible things she did, he wouldn't want to remain friends. She viewed herself as a disgusting, damaged person.

Then, she does share a few stories and tells him she knows how the world perceives someone who screws up, by saying 'People don't like drunks.' Gwen's opinion of herself is that she *is unworthy*.

Eddie replies to her: 'Those are just things you've done, they're not *who you are*. People make mistakes. Who you are is just fine, more than fine.'"

And that's what I learned in rehab, Marie, I'm just fine as a child of God," Judith states.

Marie asks, "Would you mind telling me why you ended up in rehab? If you don't want to share, I'll respect your privacy."

"I don't mind sharing with you, Marie. That's why you're here. To learn."

Judith tells Marie what happened, "Growing up I heard I was a bad girl, a horrible baby, a rotten person. The list went on and on and because I believed it, I acted out and constantly got in trouble. I identified myself with my actions. Of course, I became my own abuser by repeating that self-induced tape recording with the false and distorted messages about myself.

"I hated myself and felt unworthy of love. I numbed the pain by drinking. That's why I relate to Gwen. I denied seeing and admitting my problem. When you tie your identity to your actions, it's hard to admit you make mistakes. The ability to separate your actions from your core identity allows you to grow *through* mistakes so you don't stay stuck in the past."

Judith pauses for a moment and Marie remarks. "I think I'm beginning to understand. *I didn't realize I have let my actions define me.* Sometimes I don't like myself either. But it's because of past actions that I don't like about myself."

"You're right, Marie," Judith confirms.

Judith continues about the importance of making mistakes. "Marie, think about mistakes this way by remembering this acronym:

Many **I**mportant **S**teps **T**oward **A**cquiring **K**nowledge, **E**xperience & **S**olutions ™

There are three important points regarding mistakes:

1. Everybody makes them
2. Forgive yourself for making them, and
3. Learn from them."

Marie asks, "How does forgiving yourself help?"

Judith answers, "You can let go of perfectionism when you forgive yourself for your actions. Perfectionism puts unrealistic expectations on you. It creates the *'if only I could do better, people will like me'* people-pleasing syndrome. Nobody's perfect."

Marie lets out a big sigh and says, "You just recited my daily mantra."

They laugh.

Judith smiles, "It was my mantra too, Marie. One of my counselors shared some words of wisdom with me.

'Your beliefs, values, concepts and personal perceptions create your current level of awareness. You make all your decisions and take actions based on your present awareness. Which means you can never excel above your existing level of knowledge.'

Knowledge comes from learning. One of the ways to learn, happens when we make mistakes. I could easily forgive myself once I understood the concept behind those words. It also means I can finally forgive others for the pain they have caused me.

Forgiveness leads to seeing the silver in your treasure. It's the ultimate act of self-love which brings an inner peace to help you let go of the past.

Forgiveness doesn't mean that you deny the other person's responsibility for hurting you, and it doesn't minimize or justify the wrong. It allows you to let go of the pain and hurt so *their* past actions no longer control you. You take your power back."

Marie smiles, reflection on the meaning of power that Paul shared with her earlier.

Judith looks at Marie and says, "I see you smiling, care to share your thoughts?"

"Paul's acronym for the word power just popped into my mind;
Potential **O**ptimized **W**ith **E**xtraordinary **R**esults™"

Judith chuckles and points to the window in the front room of the cottage. A plaque hangs on the wall with those very words.

"Marie, our time together is almost over, how will you start to forgive yourself?"

Marie responds to Judith's question, "Could you give me ideas to get started?"

"Of course!" Judith exclaims. "Pull out your guidebook and open it." Marie does and notices the words 'self-love' appears on the next tab.

Judith continues, "You will write a letter of forgiveness to yourself. On the blank page, write 'I Forgive Myself.'

On the next page write 'Who I Will Forgive?' and make a list of people who you feel hurt or disappointed you.

Turn the page and write, 'Asking for Forgiveness' and make a list of people you will apologize to for your own actions. Write your letter of forgiveness first before you do the other two exercises. It can take a while for you to forgive others and tell others you are sorry. Heal yourself first by 'Polishing the Silver.'"

Marie interrupts Judith with a question, "Polishing the Silver?"

"What happens to silver Marie, if you neglect it?"

"It tarnishes," replies Marie. "The bright, shiny surface of silver gradually darkens and becomes dull."

"Yes, Marie, through polishing it with care and love, your silver stays shiny and bright. Go to the next page in your guidebook and write 'Polishing the Silver' on the top.

Here are some actions that will show love and care toward yourself.

- Stop all criticism toward yourself; stop terrorizing yourself with negative thoughts
- Treat yourself as you would treat someone you love
- Look in the mirror and say 'I love you'
- Gently change your thoughts of self-hatred to more loving ones
- Praise yourself and send love to your 'flaws'
- Give yourself a hug
- Give yourself permission to heal
- Go on a relaxing retreat
- Spend time with yourself
- Read inspirational books
- Visit someone you rarely see
- Take care of your body

You can keep adding to the list. Pick one item and do it for a day, a week or whatever feels right for you," Judith says.

Marie asks Judith what self-love action she found most useful during her recovery.

"Everyone is different. I discovered pampering myself regularly allows me to heal and grow a lifetime love affair with myself. It helps clear my mind. It's why I started The Heavenly Retreat Spa, "Judith replies.

"If I know Barb, she's already there," Marie says with a chuckle.

"Not quite," says Barb appearing unexpectedly at the door. "But I did make reservations for a facial for both of us."

"Hi, Barb and Captain, perfect timing. Come on in for a moment while I retrieve my car keys," Judith says.

"Judith, remember taking care of yourself is never called pampering," the Captain says.

"Excellent reminder." Judith answers. "It's important to watch the words one uses."

Marie, before we leave for the spa, be sure write down these three affirmations in your guidebook.

- I love and accept myself.
- I treat myself with unconditional love.
- I am perfect exactly as I am.

Seeing the good in yourself begins when you unlink your actions from your inner greatness... your true Magical Essence. Start with loving yourself. When you love yourself, you see the good all around you. You enjoy the results of your achievements.

You cannot enjoy true happiness if you are not at peace with yourself. In order to truly love another, a person needs to first love their self unconditionally. Your relationship with yourself is the most important one you'll ever experience.

Remember the words from my favorite movie, *'Those are just things you've done, not who you are. People make mistakes. Who you are is just fine, more than fine,'* Judith says to Marie.

Marie thanks Judith with a smile on her face, puts on her shoes and follows Judith, the Captain and Barb to the spa.

* *28 Days copyright 2000 Columbia Pictures (a Sony Pictures Entertainment company)*

CHAPTER 8

Tropical Storm Guilt

Barb escorts Marie into the facility. The elegance and beauty of the lobby takes Marie's breath away. A certain tranquility resonates throughout the spa. One of the aestheticians greets Judith and says, "These must be our honored guests."

"Yes," Judith replies. "Carrie, you know Barb and this is Marie. Please give them the Body Rejuvenation package."

"The Body Rejuvenation package?" Marie inquires.

"Yes, the package includes a body scrub, massage and facial with a light lunch."

Marie meets her massage therapist, Amy, in a private room. Her treatment begins with the body scrub. The delicious aroma of lavender wafts through the room and Marie begins to feel a sense of calm.

Her mind begins to wander back to the last time she tried to indulge herself and the negative response she received from Lloyd. Amy senses some tension in Marie and asks if she is scrubbing with too much pressure.

"Oh, the pressure's fine," Marie responds. "Last time I went to a spa, it resulted in an unpleasant encounter with my husband."

"Try this idea," Amy replies. "While I rub the body salt over you, visualize it rubbing away those unpleasant thoughts."

Marie accepts Amy's suggestion and quickly pushes Lloyd's critical remarks aside, reflecting on Judith's words about loving herself. She is determined to enjoy this rejuvenating experience.

Amy finishes the salt scrub and says, "Now shower yourself off and see all those negative, unpleasant thoughts going down the drain along with the salt."

Marie chuckles and takes her advice. She enjoys how soft her skin feels while she dries off. Marie returns to the room for her massage. She envisions her body soaking up self-love as the oil Amy uses absorbs into her skin.

After the massage and facial, Marie and Barb enjoy a light lunch of grilled chicken salad and fresh fruit. They finish just as Judith and the Captain drive up to the entrance. They enter the car and everyone heads to the dock. It is time for the Magical Essence to sail to the next island.

Marie hugs Judith and thanks her for the gifts asking how she can repay the kindness. "You can repay me by unconditionally loving yourself."

Everyone finishes saying their goodbyes and Judith whispers into Marie's ear, "I *believe in you.*"

Back on board the Magical Essence, Marie adds the three new affirmations Judith gave her. She opens the chest to remove the scroll and notices the appearance of several silver coins.

Barb knocks at the open door. She turns toward Barb standing in the doorway and says, "Look! Silver coins!" Barb walks toward Marie and peers into the chest.

"Yep! Those are silver coins alright. The more love you show yourself the more coins will appear," she says in response to Marie's observation.

Barb continues, "When they start to tarnish, it's a sign you are neglecting yourself."

Marie finishes writing the new affirmations on the scroll, places it in the chest and heads up to the deck. Feeling relaxed from the massage, Marie doses off on the lounger.

While asleep, the subconscious feelings she held at bay during her spa session turns into a dream. She relives a time when Barb treated Marie to a day at the spa for her birthday several years ago.

Marie felt so happy with the gift. She always wanted to spend a day at the spa and Barb knew it. She told her she needed to take better care of herself and remarked how Marie would give of herself, often putting other's happiness before hers.

Lloyd thought it was a frivolous gift. "What a waste. Like your life is so hard you need to rest up at some spa? Who do you think you are? The Queen of Sheba?!"

Marie didn't enjoy her day of pampering because she kept hearing Lloyd's negativity echoing in her subconscious making her feel guilty.

"Instead of wasting time at some silly spa, you could get caught up with things that need getting done around this house. It's a dump. What about planning the community barbecue? Aren't you in charge this year?"

Her mother's voice joined the chorus. "I don't know about this friend of yours, Marie. She's always putting wild ideas into your mind. I always put my children first. I worked hard to create a home for you and your brothers and sisters, putting *my* dreams on hold."

Marie's guilt grows as she recalls enjoying a few moments of happiness, letting someone else pamper her, and indulging in what her mother called a "decadent activity."

If they could see her now, sailing around a magical tropical ocean, being treated like royalty, abandoning her husband and daughter to indulge in the selfish pursuit of her dreams. Voices swirled around her head like the wind, saying, "Who do you think you are? What kind of mother leaves her daughter at camp so she can play 'Lifestyles of the Rich and Famous?'" Mocking words and ridicule kept swirling through her mind.

The guilt overwhelms Marie. She starts to regret feeling better about herself and shouts in her dream, "I *deserve* happiness!' There is nothing wrong with having dreams and going after them. Damn it, people do it all time. I just want to feel better about myself!"

The boat starts tossing on the waves, suddenly jolting Marie awake. Barb runs up to the deck to check on her.

"Tropical Storm Guilt is headed our way," Barb shouts. "My dad just got a warning."

Marie remembers the Captain saying her thoughts will navigate them through the ocean. As she and Barb head downstairs, she turns to Barb and asks, "Did I put us in the direction of the storm? Is this my fault?"

The Captain enters the room to see if they made it down okay and hears Marie's question.

"Marie, yes, your thoughts attracted this storm. It happens to all of us because our thoughts act like magnets, pulling energy towards us, good or bad."

Now Marie feels awful because she believes she is putting everyone's safety in jeopardy.

The Captain continues, "Do you recall, I said you would encounter storms on this trip?"

"Yes, Captain."

He continues, "We all encounter storms in our lives. You'll come out stronger when you face them and get through them. Feeling guilty is a conditioned response, not an authentic emotion, you learned to feel guilty when someone judged you repeatedly. You grew up judging yourself with unrealistic expectations."

Marie chimes in, "I'm feeling guilty about several things. Contemplating divorcing Lloyd, being away from my daughter, interfering with your trip. Even all the attention I'm receiving. I don't know why you're doing all this for me."

"Because you're *worth* it," the Captain reassures her. "Guilt is the only human emotion requiring your consent to thrive. In other words, you *surrender* your power over to it.

Guilt is a form of manipulation and the greatest destroyer of emotional energy. It leaves you feeling immobilized in the present by something that occurred long ago. If you hang onto it, it will keep you from moving forward in a positive and productive way. It's a form of inner conflict and you lose no matter what you do. You must remove it from your life!

Guilt can't exist without your permission. What do you think you need to do to take back your power from guilt?"

Marie ponders what the Captain shares with her and replies. "If this is a response to me judging myself with unrealistic expectations, then I must stop criticizing and judging myself. Judith gave me the perfect solution: love and accept myself, treat myself with unconditional love and realize I am perfect exactly as I am.

I forgive myself for giving guilt control over my life. When I notice it taking over, I need to acknowledge my response, change my thoughts and become conscious when I judge and compare myself."

"Wow!" Barb exclaims.

"You got it, Marie. And may I offer a couple of suggestions?" the Captain asks.

"Of course."

"Use the 'Polish the Silver' self-love suggestions Judith gave you whenever guilt decides to visit. Loving yourself doesn't feel natural to you yet and guilt and unkind thoughts can easily sneak back into your life.

"Write down the thoughts and words that brought this storm to us in the 'Thoughts Section' of your guidebook. Especially while they are fresh in your mind."

"I'll do it now," she says. Shifting her mind to more pleasant thoughts, they watch the waves calm down as the storm breaks up. The sun soon returns to shine on them again.

"Okay Marie, let's get back on course. Focus on your dream, your promise and let those thoughts guide us to the next island," the Captain tells her.

"Aye, Aye, Captain." Marie looks at the compass and notices it pointing to True ME.

"Great, we can move in the right direction again," says the Captain, "Look! You'll see the Island of Gratitude just over the horizon."

CHAPTER 9

Step 4 - Island of Gratitude

Marie follows the Captain's suggestion. She opens the "Self-Love Section" of the Guidebook and selects from the 'self-love list', 'Look in the mirror and say I Love You.'

Marie walks over to the mirror and looks deeply into her own eyes and says, "I love you." Her voice cracks while repeating the phrase several times. Eventually she smiles back at herself.

She turns to the "Thoughts Section" and writes down the unpleasant thoughts from her dream. Doing the exercise feels as if l someone opened a spigot, and a flood of limiting beliefs and put-downs directed toward her, over the years, come gushing out. She can't write fast enough.

She notices something miraculous happening. Instead of accepting the self-limiting words and beliefs she finds herself *disagreeing* with them for the very first time.

She goes back up to the deck as the Magical Essence docks at the Island of Gratitude. With everything secured, the Captain, Barb and Marie disembark, making their way up the merchant-lined street.

Stopping in front of one of the shops, Marie notices the lettering on the window, "M.W. Imagination Graphics Studio." The Captain opens the door and motions for Barb and Marie to enter. He follows, closing the door behind him.

A man with receding salt-and-pepper hair greets them. His gentle smile reveals laugh lines around his blue-grey eyes. The Captain introduces Marie to Marcus Wallace, owner of the studio.

"Why don't we sit down?" Marcus asks while motioning to a sitting area in the studio.

Everyone takes a seat to catch up on what's happened since the last time Barb, her father and Marcus met. At this point, the Captain says, "Marie, Barb and I are going to leave you in Marcus's capable hands. We made other plans for us during this part of the trip"

"Enjoy yourselves," Marie says.

"When you finish, you will find us right here waiting," Marcus replies.

When Barb and her father leave, Marcus turns to Marie and says, "My cup could use a refill, would you like one?"

"Yes, I would," Marie replies.

She looks at a beautifully designed lithograph hanging on the wall with the quote *"Gratitude is the Master Key that Opens All Doors of Possibility" ~ Stacey Robyn*

"Oh, I like that quote," Marie says pointing to the artwork.

"It's a philosophy I live by," Marcus comments. "An important lesson in life I learned years ago. I was miserable and chronically complained about every aspect of my life. Unappreciative of everything, I stressed out about paying the bills and clients seemed to dry up. Nothing worked to bring in new business and I ended up in the hospital with a heart attack.

My roommate turned out to be a God-send. Years earlier he had lost everything through a freak accident. At first, bitterness and anger filled his heart. He told me he never appreciated what he had until it was gone. He began to appreciate his life when it occurred to him it could all be taken away. He's thankful for a second chance.

His words made me think I could have died too, but I didn't. An epiphany occurred to me. God owns everything. It all belongs to him. He entrusts me with what He gives me.

I decided to follow my roommate's example and started writing down all the things God gave and gives me. I started the list with these words. 'I wonder why God has blessed me with this...'

I do this because all blessings come with a purpose and responsibility and not to take them for granted. It keeps me aware of how I can use my blessings to better my life and those around me.

I know God truly gave me a second chance to turn my life around after the heart attack. Every morning I start my day with appreciation by writing five things I'm grateful for. Sometimes I'm simply grateful I woke up in the morning. I thank God for new clients, great interns, the sun rising. I feel expressing Gratitude is so important."

"I'm glad you survived your heart attack. Do you really write every morning?" Marie asks.

"Thank you, and yes," Marcus says. "Let me continue telling you about the Power of Gratitude. It can make you satisfied with your surroundings without feeling like you are settling for less. There is a difference. Gratitude keeps you connected to Universal Source which provides you with everything you need. This helps you stay open to receiving abundance.

Settling indicates a scarcity or *lack* mentality by not believing in the unlimited resources available to you.

Gratitude on the other hand, will expand your abundance attraction mentality. Expressing appreciation for what you currently possess, no matter how small or simple, allows you to happily enjoy today. It keeps you open to the benefits you'll receive in the future.

The dreams you wrote, from your heart, in the Ocean of Possibilities Guidebook, brought you here, correct?"

Marie answers, "Correct. I guess you did something similar, didn't you?"

"Yes, Marie. I discovered the importance of knowing what I want gives me clarity in life. Without it, I would drift around in uncertainty, which can feel empty and frustrating. But dreams also serve another important function."

He continues, "God doesn't give us an idea or dream without giving us everything we need to see it realized. Your dreams, desires and ideas are there for you to use to harness the inner gifts, talents and assets He gave you.

He placed those dreams in your life to find joy, happiness, self-expression and fulfillment. When you pursue them, your authentic self freely expresses and expands your full potential.

Think of your gifts, natural talents, and assets as gems. Those gems represent self-confidence, a very necessary ingredient required to release your inner success.

Gratitude isn't just for receiving material things. You show gratitude by believing in and using your natural talents and gifts. Using your gifts builds your self-confidence, which is perhaps the most important quality, because self-confidence is what sets those who live up to their potential apart from those who don't.

When you came into this world, your gems start out as rough, unpolished stones. Using your talents, abilities and skills polishes and shapes them. Just like a gemologist turns rough stones into sparkling gems, the more you use them, the more they shine."

Marcus pauses and asks Marie to share her thoughts.

Marie responds, "I was just thinking about what Judith shared with me about separating past actions from my authentic self and how it affects my self-worth. One of the reasons I hesitated in the past came from the fear of failure. For me to polish my gifts and build my confidence, I need to realize I will make MISTAKES. It's an important part of the growing and learning process.

I'm beginning to see how everything is connecting, starting with seeing and believing in my self-worth. I am a *worthy* person just because I exist. That's really the first critical step to living the life I desire and to experience the success I want in life."

Marcus nods his head, "Yes, you're a fast learner, Marie. Belief in yourself builds when you begin to accept and own your talents and abilities. Gaining faith in your innate skills will release the success within you.

My coffee cup could use a refill, what about you?" Marcus asks.

"Yes, please," Marie agrees as they head toward the break room.

Marcus continues the conversation, "You will find self-confidence present in people **before** they become successful. Once they start working toward success, these traits run parallel, each fueling the other. Self-confidence positively recharges your mind."

Marcus pours the coffee, "Your growing confidence will support you at each step as you proceed towards success. And as you experience more success, your self-confidence will increase. It is important to develop a harmonious relationship between your confidence levels and the journey you take to experience the success you desire.

Let me ask you four questions to help you explore your self-confidence."

"Sure, Marcus," Marie replies.

"Marie, first I am asking you to open the guidebook to the *'Polishing Your Gemstones of Confidence'* section."

Marie chuckles and says, "I love this guidebook and how all the right sections magically appear. I see a Gratitude List section too."

Marcus's blue-grey eyes twinkle when he smiles saying, "You don't need to answer these questions right now, you may want to think about them and write your answers later.

Are you grateful for your God-given gifts?

Next, are you using those gifts?"

Marie shakes her head, and responds she has never thought about it. Marcus continued with the next question.

3. "Are you comfortable accepting compliments?"

Marcus notices Marie looking uncomfortable with the question, so he elaborates.

"We often downplay compliments, especially a compliment about something that comes naturally to us. Remember this: When somebody gives you the gift of a compliment and you refuse it, you block yourself from *receiving a gift* and you are blocking them from *giving that gift*. This causes you to break the cycle of circulation, one of the universal principles of abundance and prosperity.

When someone gives you a genuine compliment, you need to thank them."

"I never thought of it that way, Marcus," Marie replies. "I guess when you don't feel good about yourself, it's hard to accept when somebody is saying something nice to you. Receiving compliments makes me feel uncomfortable."

"Marie, you are expressing a common reaction to accepting compliments. Keep practicing by saying thank you and you'll get comfortable with receiving them. Especially if you remember how its grounded in the law of circulation.

Now the final question: What are the talents and assets you downplay? Thinking about past compliments you've received over the years can give you some hints."

"Gee Marcus, what if I don't know how to recognize my natural talents?"

"Marie, you'll find additional questions in the Guidebook to help you connect with your inner abilities.

You and I are here for a purpose, to accomplish our life's work and realize our true potential. If you ignore and deny your true self, it can cause *stress, anxiety and depression*, leaving you with the feeling something is missing in your life. When you feel this way, it's hard to feel grateful.

Start your gratitude list by writing in your Guidebook at least 100 things you appreciative in your life."

Marcus notices Marie's eyes grow wide. Taking a sip of his coffee, he says, "Now this may seem daunting. It's easy to list the obviously big items. You may find that eventually your mind will run out of things to write.

"That's when it's important to appreciate the little everyday mundane things, that you may be taking for granted. Things like a good night's sleep, getting green lights when you're in a hurry, or having clean water to drink. Are you getting the idea?" Marcus asks.

Marie nods in agreement.

"This exercise provides the jumpstart need to live a life of gratitude. Once you complete writing the 100 items, continue to add to the list daily with five more things you appreciate."

Barb and her father enter into the studio and join Marcus and Marie in the seating area. "How's it going Marcus?" asks the Captain.

"I believe our time together went very well. Marie is a fast-learner. I'm grateful for the opportunity to meet her and share the wisdom I've gained through my own experiences," Marcus replies.

"I agree, Captain," Marie says. "He gave me plenty to ponder, especially about being grateful for my gifts and abilities. They are the gems of developing my self-confidence. Marcus helped me see personal compliments in a completely different light. Now I need to figure out how to embrace my natural talents."

"That's fabulous, Marie. And we now need to be on our way. Marcus, thanks for taking time out of your day for Marie," the Captain says.

"My pleasure," he replies.

Marcus hands her a card with three new affirmations to write on her scroll. He hugs her and says, "You can do it, it's in you. Take time to think about your natural talents. I *believe in you*."

As they return to the boat, Marie notices a craft shop and asks Barb if she would mind stopping in.

"Great idea," Barb says. "Dad, is it okay with you?"

"Of course, you two enjoy yourselves and I'll see you back at the boat," Captain T replies.

They enter the store and notice, on the right side, brightly colored bolts of fabric lining the wall. Barb, who enjoys knitting, quickly finds skeins of yarn.

Marie notices the jewelry-making section near the window. The sunlight streaming bouncing off the beads and rhinestones reflects sparkling patterns on the wall. Looking at the beads, great ideas come to her for several pieces, including thank you gifts for Barb and Captain T.

Barb finishes selecting her yarns and joins Marie.

Marie looks at Barb and hesitates briefly before saying, then she says, "When I was a little girl, I always loved jewelry, especially making it. I would sketch pictures of my designs and created designer collections for my Barbie dolls. I enjoyed making the jewelry for my dolls more than I did playing with them. They modeled the most elaborate jewelry of all the dolls on the block. This is something I always wanted to do...design jewelry."

"I often remarked on the beautiful pieces you made over the years. I figured it was a hobby like my knitting is for me. This is your *dream*, isn't it?" Barb asks.

"Yes, it's what I shared with Regina on the Island of Hope. Growing up, I always saw myself as a famous jewelry designer," Marie replies.

"It's one of your natural talents," Barb affirms.

On the way to the counter, Marie discovers a tote bag she must have. "I can put my jewelry items and tools in it, along with my Guidebook," she says to Barb.

Barb remarks, "Look at all the pockets inside and out. I'm grabbing one too."

Despite Barb's protest, Marie purchases Barb's items, giving a wink and saying, "Let me do something for *you*."

They arrive back to the Magical Essence. The boat heads toward the next island. Later, while casually dining on the deck, Captain T tells them they'll reach the island by morning. At the end of the meal, Marie asks if they would excuse her because she'd like to devote time to contemplating the wisdom Marcus shared with her.

The Captain and Barb wish her goodnight. Marie opens the Guidebook and reads the four questions Marcus asked her earlier.

Self Confidence Exploration Questions:

- Are you grateful for your God-given gifts?
- Are you using your gifts?
- Are you comfortable accepting compliments?
- What talents and assets do you downplay?

Marie focuses fully on answering the questions in detail, especially the last one.

Before getting ready for bed, she begins her appreciation list. She opens her chest to add the three new affirmations to her evening routine. And she delights in noticing new gemstones appeared in her treasure chest in various forms - from uncut to polished.

"I guess I've already developed and used some of my gifts and didn't even know it," she says to herself.

Marie writes the following affirmations.

- I am willing to see my own magnificence.
- I think and speak positively.
- I accept all parts of myself.

She starts writing her gratitude list. This profound exercise opens her eyes to see the many ways God is already blessing her life. She thinks about Captain T's words, "You can live the life you so richly deserve." Marie, believes *it's already happening.*

She feels a sense of inner peace and calmness she never experienced before. Could gratitude already cause this significant shift? She texts Elizabeth to let her know how much she loves and appreciates her.

Marie drifts easily off to sleep, looking forward to visiting the Island of Courage in the morning.

Time to claim another item on your treasure hunt. You'll find it at www.annrusnak.com/gems

CHAPTER 10

Step 5 - Island of Courage

Marie wakes up and joins Barb and her father in the main salon of the Magical Essence.

"Do you feel better this morning?" Barb asks.

"Yes, I do, and even feel better about myself. Thanks for asking," she replies. "What Marcus said about expressing gratitude for the gifts and talents given to me, helped me see myself in a different light. Those things are part of what makes me…ME! There is nothing *wrong* with me."

Sitting in front of the coffee table, Marie looks at the parchment map of the Ocean of Possibilities. Something about the arrangement of the islands reminds her of a stepping stone pathway. She recalls an ancient Chinese proverb and shares, "A journey of a thousand miles begins with a single step."

"I can see the logic of the islands we visited so far and how they form the steps toward opening my heart's desires.

The first step is Hope. It all starts with hope, but if I don't take responsibility for my life, hope turns into hopelessness. The second is taking Responsibility for my thoughts, actions and outcomes. I can do this because of the third step, Forgiveness. I can love my true self, even if I make mistakes, because we can forgive mistakes and learn from them. This gives me the freedom to develop my natural abilities, my talents and gifts, build my confidence and stay connected to source, my creator, through the fourth step of Gratitude."

"Marie, What a *profound* observation. The 'Chart Your Course' vision you wrote truly came from your heart's desire," the Captain responds.

"I agree," Barb says.

"Designing jewelry is the childhood dream my parents discouraged me from pursuing. But a new dream came into my life with the birth of my daughter. She became the priority. Now I feel something deep inside driving me to continue taking the next steps toward living a more fulfilling life."

"You're going to enjoy meeting your next mentor, DelaRose," Barb replies as they cruise into the harbor.

"Can't wait," Marie says.

They dock, disembark and walk to "DelaRose Expressions Boutique." The threesome enters the shop together.

A pretty mocha-skinned woman waves and calls out to them. "Hello, Captain T and Barb," she says with a Jamaican accent. Wearing a white tank top and plaid rose-hued quadrille skirt on her ample frame.

Her head wrap matches the skirt and she's accented her outfit with a colorful beaded necklace, bangles and large gold hoop earrings.

She gives Marie a warm smile saying, "This must be my protégé. Welcome to the Island of Courage."

"Yes, it is," the Captain says as he introduces her to Marie.

"Pleasure meeting you, DelaRose," Marie says extending her hand.

"Let's dispense with the formalities and give me a hug if you feel comfortable, Marie."

Marie hugs DelaRose, who then turns to Barb and asks, "How did the outfit work out for your Fourth of July party?"

"Rave after rave. What a fashion hit," Barb answers.

"So, this is where you got that fabulous outfit!" Marie exclaims.

Barb replies with sly grin while placing her index finger over her lips in a 'shhh' motion. "Yes, and now you know my secret shopping place."

Marie looks closer at DelaRose's necklace and notices the different colorful shapes aren't beads.

"What type of gems are on your necklace? It's gorgeous. I don't recall ever seeing them before," Marie inquires.

"Natural pearls, Marie. And like me, each one is unique and not perfectly shaped," DelaRose says confidently with a full body chuckle.

"Captain T, I will take Marie for a walk now, so I hope you came prepared with something to do. I know Barb will keep herself amused shopping through my creations," DelaRose says as she puts her arm around Marie.

"Don't worry, DelaRose. You know me, always got something to do. And I know my daughter could spend *days* in your shop."

"Oh, Dad," a smiling Barb responds. "I'll see you, Marie, after your visit."

With her arm locked in Marie's, DelaRose says, "Come and walk with me to my private secret garden."

"Secret garden?"

"Yes, Marie, my special place of refuge. A haven. My oasis from the day-to-day drudgery. A place where I go into solitude to connect with my inner creator."

They walk for a short distance, close to the ocean, and enter a garden of tropical flowers. A beautiful wooden gazebo painted white stand majestically in the center of the garden. DelaRose invites Marie into the gazebo. They sit and make themselves comfortable.

"I'm glad you noticed my necklace, Marie. I wear the natural pearls to remind me to see my self-worth and hold myself in high-esteem.

"The potential to achieve your most desired dreams comes from your level of self-esteem. It's important for you to have a good opinion of yourself to see yourself as worthy of success."

Marie focuses on the beauty of the hibiscus flowers behind DelaRose, nodding in agreement while listening intently.

"Your self-esteem is represented by the 'natural' pearls in your treasure chest."

"I think I'm seeing a pattern here," Marie remarks.

"Silver showed up when I started loving myself by forgiving myself. The colorful gems showed up when I started to feel more confident in my natural abilities and talents and began giving thanks for everything in my life.

"Now, you will show me how pearls will show up in my treasure chest. Correct? I bet courage plays an important part."

DelaRose chuckles and says, "Yes, but you're jumping ahead.

"Did you know the pearl is the only jewel that can be worn in its natural state? It needs no polishing or cutting to bring out its beauty. Pearls are found in one out of every 10,000 oysters. Their sheer rarity drives their value to the highest levels above other gems with one exception, the diamond.

I love this quote from the great gemologist, George Fredrick Kunz. He says, *'The pearl owes nothing to man. It is absolutely a gift of nature on which man cannot improve.'*

You won't find perfectly shaped *natural* pearls. It is this individuality that makes them unique. Designed by nature with no human interference."

Marie makes a comment, "I didn't know that about pearls. What about cultured pearls? Is a *cultured* pearl real?"

"Yes, in a way. Let me explain," DelaRose continues.

"A *cultured* pearl can still be considered 'natural' because Mother Nature creates them, but human intervention influences the process, by using irritants inserted into the oyster.

While natural pearls come in a wide variety of shapes, sizes, and qualities, cultured pearls can be 'designed' as round or any desired shape."

DelaRose notices the quizzical look on Marie's face. She pulls two pearls from her skirt pocket and holds them in her palm for Marie to see.

"The exteriors of a natural and cultured pearl look identical. Don't you agree?"

"I agree," Marie says nodding her head

Pointing to the two pearls, DelaRose continues, "Only an x-ray provides the definitive way to tell the two apart. Only from the inside can you tell whether a pearl is natural or cultured.

Think of the irritant of negativity we may all endure from parents, friends and family This human intervention can turn anyone into a *cultured* pearl. Those 'irritants' prevent us from seeing the worth of your authentic natural self."

A human 'cultured pearl' is formed by those who hold to society's 'norms' and who tell others how they should be, how they should think, act and behave. Even what they should believe."

Marie sighs deeply, her doleful eyes focusing on DelaRose's necklace.

"How do you think you see yourself, cultured or natural, Marie?" DelaRose asks.

Looking downcast, Marie quietly answers, "Cultured. My whole life has been based on what other people told me about who I am. But recently, for my daughter's sake, I began questioning those beliefs and expectations."

"Marie, it takes courage to go against society, to go against your parent's teachings. You did a *courageous* thing going on this journey. It will take a lot of fortitude to remove the cultured pearls from your treasure chest and replace them with natural ones."

DelaRose shares, "The person who is able to authentically be themselves is *empowered and dauntless*. They will risk rejection while standing up for who they are."

A sullen look appears on Marie's face as she looks up.

In a cheerful, hopeful tone, DelaRose encouragingly says, "When you decide to nurture and embrace your true essence, you'll learn to love yourself unconditionally. You won't need to deny who you naturally are in order to receive love from others. You'll feel good about yourself. People will seek you out because you won't fear rejection, or worry about what others think."

Marie starts, "It sounds wonderful, like an inner peace will come to me. The same inner peace and happiness I noticed I felt after being with my other mentors. I noted your confidence the moment I saw you. You just radiate self-assurance."

DelaRose smiles and places the cultured pearl in Marie's hand. Marie looks at it and starts to twirl it between her two fingers. She looks up at DelaRose and asks, "How do I go about increasing my self-esteem so I can replace the cultured pearls? With natural ones like your necklace?"

DelaRose answers her, "It took years to shift and change my thinking processes away from all those 'cultural' beliefs and habits. You will need to go deep inside, connect with the natural 'you' and discover your potential. I will walk you through an exercise called the 'Future You.'

Success begins in your mindset. Accepting and seeing yourself already successful is critical. First, the mind needs to see it before you can *achieve* it. Your attitude affects your actions. Your actions produce your results.

"Are you ready?" she asks Marie.

"Yes, DelaRose, I am."

"Marie, close your eyes," she says.

Marie closes her eyes and listens to the ocean waves. Her breathing becomes slow and relaxed. DelaRose continues. "Take a deep breath in and let it out slowly. See yourself in a theatre. Find a comfortable seat. In front you, see three big screens. They are illuminated. Look at all three. Dim the screens except for the first one… leave the light shining on it.

A movie begins to play on Screen One… It's titled "THE FUTURE YOU"… you see a person on the screen. It is you… a year from today.

Look at the future you on the screen:

- How do you look?
- Do you look different?
- Notice your weight, your hair, your clothes…how are you dressed?
- How is your posture? Does it show authority?
- Are you warm and friendly?
- Is the future you self-confident or filled with self-doubt?
- Does the person on the screen project trust, respect and admiration?
- Is the future you a follower or leader?

What is the message the future you is sending? *What is the difference between the future you and the present you?*

Look at the future you one more time… what's the one word that describes the future you on Screen One? Remember that word.

Now dim that screen and bring the second screen into focus.

A movie begins to play on Screen Two… Its title is 'YOUR FUTURE WORK ENVIRONMENT'… you see your future work environment on the screen…it's your office a year from now.

Look around your office…

- What is the atmosphere like in your office?
- Does it feel energetic… positive… an environment that creates success?
- Look at your furniture… notice your desk… is it cluttered with piles of paper or neatly organized?
- Do you enjoy your work? What is your stress level?
- Do you work alone or have a support staff?
- Are you reactive or proactive to situations?

Is the future *you* still dealing with the same problems that prevent you from achieving your desired results today?

What is the message your future work environment is sending? What is the difference between it and your present work place?

"Look over your future work environment on Screen Two one more time… what's the one word that describes it? Make a mental note of the word.

Now dim Screen Two and shine the light on Screen Three… focus on the third screen.

A movie begins to play on Screen Three… Its title is 'ENJOYING LIFE'… you see a future vacation playing on the screen… it's your vacation in the near future.

Picture yourself on vacation.

- Where are you?
- What noises do you hear?
- What aromas do you smell?
- Who is with you on this vacation?
- Can you separate yourself from work? Did you bring work along?
- Do you give undivided attention to those around you?
- Were you able to easily afford this vacation?
- Who is taking care of everyday activities at the office while you're on vacation?
- Did the future you build your business into an organization?

What is the message you receive from this vacation? How was this vacation different from your past vacations?

"Look over your vacation on Screen Three one more time… what's the one word that describes your future vacation?

Display that word on the screen… leave the screen in view while you bring the other two screens in focus. All three screens are now visible. Screens One and Two are blank.

Look at Screen One… now you see it display the one word you used to describe the future 'you.'

Look at Screen Two…it now displays the one word you used to describe your future work environment.

All three screens feature your one-word description. Now open your eyes."

Marie opens her eyes and DelaRose hands her a card with three rectangles printed on it.

"Marie, write your three words down on the card."

Marie writes out the three words and DelaRose gives her three more cards. She looks at them and notices that each one represents one of the three screens.

Screen One card list three questions:

1. Why is the word on Screen One important to you?
2. What's the relationship between Screens One & Two?
3. What's the difference between the future you and the present you?

Card for Screen Two:

1. Why is the word on Screen Two important to you?
2. What's the relationship between Screens Two & Three?
3. What's the difference between your 'future work environment' and 'your present work environment?'

Card for Screen Three:

1. Why is the word on Screen Three important to you?
2. What's the relationship between Screens Three & One?
3. What's the difference between your future vacation/life and your present vacation/life?

DelaRose gives her instructions about each of the three cards. She is to answer the questions based on what she saw and felt during all three movies. Marie takes a few moments to fill out the cards.

DelaRose then instructs her to take the first card - the one with the three rectangles, flip it over and answer these three questions:

1. Did you notice a common theme between the three movie words?
2. What did you learn from watching the three movies?
3. What's one inspired action step you can take now to make your future a reality?

Marie writes the answers to the questions. She notices how this exercise helps her to see her true self.

After completing the written exercise, Marie remarks to DelaRose, "I found this exercise insightful. I liked the person I saw, someone worthy of her dreams. The person waiting for me to courageously and boldly step into myself and accept my worth."

"Marie, you can use this meditation any time you need it. A word of caution, though: Some people will show displeasure with the changes you will make so you can to live life on your terms. They will do anything to sabotage you, even family members and the people you believe love you the most.

Open your guidebook," DelaRose tells Marie. She opens it and sees "The Future You" section now in the book with pages that duplicate the cards. She tells Marie to put the cards in the back pocket of the Guidebook and transfer them later.

"Let's head back to the boutique," DelaRose says. "I want to give you an audio recording of 'The Future You' meditation to use along with your Guidebook. I recommend doing this exercise at least once a week."

"DelaRose, thanks so much," Marie says with much gratitude.

Barb is at the counter paying for her purchases, when Marie and DelaRose enter the boutique.

"Ah, just in time," Barb says. "My dad is waiting for us on the boat and I could use some help carrying these bags."

"It is an honor to help you," Marie says.

"Barb, it gives me great pleasure seeing you enjoy my artistic fashions," DelaRose said smiling. "Before you leave, I want to give Marie a gift. Come back to my office, Marie."

Marie follows DelaRose to her office where she gives her 'The Future You' audio CD with three affirmations on the cover:

- This year I do the mental work for positive change
- I am my own unique self

- I am a natural winner

"Marie, add these affirmations to your scroll."
"I will," she says.
"One more thing." DelaRose gives her a small wrapped gift box. Marie opens it and gasps.
"Oh my! Normally I would say I couldn't accept it, but I learned gratitude includes staying open to *receiving*. Thank you so much, DelaRose. Can you help me put it on?"
"Of course, Marie," DelaRose replies, clasping the natural pearl necklace around her neck.
"It's gorgeous," Marie says admiring it the mirror.
"Remember you are a *natural* pearl, rare and unique."
Marie and DelaRose grab Barb's bags. Marie cherishes the walk back to the boat as she and her friend take their time chatting. Captain T waits for them on the dock and helps them with the bags. Then he signals the crew to place them in Barb's room.
Everyone exchanges goodbyes and Marie gives DelaRose a hug. A warm feeling floods her heart when DelaRose whispers in her ear, "*I believe in you.*"
Marie enters her room and opens the treasure chest to remove the scroll and writes the new affirmations. She notices new beautiful, luminescent pearls among the gems and silver. While the majority of them appear cultured, she recognizes a few natural ones by their unique shapes, sizes and colors.
She senses a change beginning to take hold within her consciousness and it feels good.
As the sound of the boat's motor signals the Magical Essence is again on its way, Marie catches her reflection in the mirror and stops to admire the pearl necklace. Looking into her eyes, she acknowledges how much courage it takes to love herself unconditionally.

CHAPTER 11

Step 6 - Island of Trust & Faith

Barb walks into Marie's room holding several shopping bags. "You didn't think all these bags were for me, did you?" Barb inquires.

They both start laughing.

Barb continues, "We will dock and spend the rest of the day and evening at the Island of Trust and Faith. My dad and I always eat dinner at the Turquoise Waters Restaurant on the beach. They set up the tables for an oceanfront dining experience to watch the sunset as the stars appear overhead."

"That sounds wonderful," Marie chimes in.

"I bought you a dress for dinner tonight, plus some other stuff," Barb confesses.

Marie looks in the bag Barb hands her and pulls out a teal green sundress. "This goes with the pearl necklace DelaRose gave me," she says with a giggle.

Smiling, Barb hands her the other bag containing a shawl and teal colored strappy sandals.

"Oh Barb, how *beautiful*. Thank you so much. I appreciate our friendship and hope one day I can repay your kindness."

"You don't need to worry about 'repaying me.' That's the thing about giving. It always comes back to you tenfold, but not always from the original source. This way you can give for the sake of giving and let it go. Trust the Universe on how, when and where it comes back."

"That's beautiful, Barb."

The friends relax on the deck, enjoying each other's company over glasses of cold water infused with lemon and cucumber. Soon mountains appear on the horizon, as the next island comes into view.

The boat approaches the harbor dock for its stay on the island. Marie admires the beauty with its mountainous interior and coastal exterior. The gorgeous beaches shimmer like diamonds in the sun.

At the end of the dock, two women signal to them, their auburn hair blowing in the gentle tropical breeze. As they get closer, Marie notices they are identical twins, yet each expressing her own identity.

"Marie, meet Stephanie and Rai," the Captain says introducing them.

Stephanie reminds her of a 70's flower child while Rai looks ready to go on a jungle safari.

"Pleasure meeting you, Stephanie and Rai," Marie comments.

"Pleasure meeting you too, Marie," the twins say in unison.

Everyone walks from the dock to the connected oceanfront boardwalk and over to the parking lot, where Rai and Stephanie's jeep awaits them.

Marie notices the bright and colorful "Fun Beginnings in the Canopy" logo on the side of the jeep with the subtitle, "Experience World Class Romantic Eco-Ventures" under the logo.

"Romantic Eco-Ventures?" Marie asks inquisitively.

"Yes!" the twins reply in unison, "We specialize in performing weddings in the tropical forest canopy," Stephanie continues.

"Wow," replies Marie, "I never heard of anyone doing eco-weddings. How did you come up with the idea?"

"It's an amazing story," Barb replies.

Stephanie turns around and hands her backseat guests a basket filled with various sunscreens and suggests they lather on some lotion. "The sun can be intense. Last thing you want is a sunburn during our drive back to the lodge."

Everyone grabs a tube and begins applying lotion, while Stephanie shares their story. "Rai came up with the idea to purchase this company when she learned the owner wanted to sell it."

Rai chimes in, "I just love spending time outdoors, especially in the forest. I gave bus tours around the island for one of the tour companies. When I heard about this opportunity something tugged at me and wouldn't let go. After work, I headed to Stephanie's floral shop at closing time. I told her I wanted to purchase it."

"Yeah," said Stephanie, "I thought this was another one of her crazy ideas. I suggested we grab some takeout and head over to Seaside Park off the boardwalk to talk about it. Once we sat down, I noticed a difference in Rai. I could feel and hear the passion in her voice. Next thing I knew, three hours passed and the sun already set, but we didn't notice. We could barely see the ideas we scribbled all over the cocktail napkins and take out bags.

We decided to let the idea settle with a good night's sleep, and in the morning, see where our inner guidance took us. We came back to the park the next morning to continue the discussion over breakfast."

Rai continues, "The next morning we discovered neither one of us got any sleep because we were so excited. This business combined something we both desired to do for a long time. I always loved the tropical forest and Stephanie's floral shop specialized in designing floral arrangements for weddings. In addition, she become an ordained minister so she could marry the couples."

Stephanie says, "Our instincts guided us to move forward with this dream. If there's anything Rai and I have learned, it's to trust our instincts knowing the Universe never gives you a dream *without the resources to make it happen.*"

"Faith and trust combine to make you *unstoppable* when pursuing an inspired dream," Ria adds.

The jeep pulls up in front of a breathtakingly beautiful lodge which blends in perfectly with the forest surroundings. While most of the forest and mountains are locate in the center of the island, this section of the rainforest is near to the ocean, flanking the mouth of the small creek that flows down from the mountains.

As they get out of the jeep, Stephanie points to the pristine shore where a few sun worshipers are lounging, enjoying a dip in the ocean. She says, "The staff will transform the beachfront into the 'Turquoise Waters' restaurant, where you will dine tonight."

Marie is lost for words as one of the staff members takes their luggage. The beauty and tranquility of the place overwhelms her.

"Come, lunch is served in the pavilion," says Rai. The outdoor restaurant overlooks the beautiful creek next to it. The surrounding rainforest replaces the walls and windows.

Once everyone returns from the buffet and is seated, Marie remarks. "Boy, this place must have cost a fortune to buy."

"It didn't look anything like this at that time," Rai replies. "It consisted of a small rundown building where people gathered to begin the trek to the zip line. The owner filed for bankruptcy because he couldn't compete with the two other eco-venture companies.

"We didn't have money just laying around to purchase it and the banks refused to give us a business loan. Our friends told us we were crazy. Our family wouldn't help because they thought they'd be throwing their money away. People told us that it wasn't a female-friendly business. They said this island couldn't support another eco-venture company."

"The odds were against us," Rai adds.

"We believed and put faith in our vision," Stephanie states. "This dream came from our *hearts*. We trusted the Divine Spirit would guide us and provide what we would need to make this dream happen because we know it resides within us. We just need to listen, trust and take inspired action."

"We learned how faith is the connection from your head to your heart. Trust is faith in action. Through experience we discovered this is true. **Your heart is where your destiny starts and the thoughts you choose will affect your decisions and everything you do**," says Rai.

"We remained determined to make this happen. We believed the Divine Spirit would take care of the details regarding *how* it would happen. That's the Universe's job…the how," Stephanie says.

A waitress comes over to clear their empty plates.

Stephanie continues, "Rai felt guided to sell her home. And I decided to sell the flower shop and we both maxed out our credit cards. The owner worked with us to take over his loan. We still needed money to remodel the building and repair old equipment. We decided to pitch a tent on the property to cut back on living expenses.

"We kept stepping out on faith, taking inspired action and trusting all would be well."

Rai keeps the conversation going, "A very successful business owner vacationing on the island heard about our idea. He loved it and took us under his wing, mentoring us by sharing his wisdom and business acumen."

"Wow!" said a wide-eyed Marie.

"You'll love the rest of the story, Marie," Rai replies and continues. "Another young man offered his architectural services pro bono. He recently graduated and wanted to establish himself with a portfolio featuring eco-friendly designs. He designed the lodge to sit on stilts to make the smallest impact on the forest floor. He took the same concept and put the cabins on higher stilts so it feels like you're living in the trees. Each cabin comes with your very own walkway leading you to your front door." Rai motions her hand toward the walkways.

"If you don't want to zip line to the chapel tree house, he also designed a covered walkway that gracefully blends into the environment. He even designed the deluxe treehouses where you will stay tonight. You wi8ll experience the off-the-ground walkways on the way to your lodgings."

The chatter from a pair of howler monkeys, playing near the pavilion, interrupts the conversation and everyone laughs.

Stephanie points to a wall of plaques near the buffet station, picking up the story, "The architect earned several rewards for his eco-friendly designs which helped launch his very successful career in San Francisco. The Divine Spirit truly made this dream come true. We kept following our inner guidance, our own Magical Essence, not knowing the next step to take until it was shown to us. This place turned out bigger and better than we imagined."

"Weren't you scared? Didn't you have doubts?" Marie asks concern on her face. "I can't even imagine doing what you did. Giving up jobs, selling your homes and business without knowing how to make it all happen."

"Sure, Marie, you have to believe you're *worthy of your dreams.* Captain T taught us we're worthy just because we're children of the Universe. You must believe in the dreams coming from your heart," Rai says as she puts her hand over her heart.

"It takes courage to follow your dreams and step into your destiny. Eventually, you learn to believe and trust the best way will show itself. For example, after several months, ideas came to us on how we could raise the money. We took the action and it worked out. But it doesn't happen overnight."

Marie, looking in awe, places her elbows on the table, perching her chin on her hands.

Stephanie shares a secret with her, "Every time fear tried to enter my heart and my thoughts, it signaled I had misplaced my faith. To reconnect to Divine Spirit, I would visualize holding a starfish in my hand, seeing it shine the way to my inner guidance. Fear can't stand up to Faith and Trust, the two most powerful weapons against fear and doubt."

"A starfish?" Marie inquires with a puzzled look on her face.

"Yes, our grandmother told us the Starfish Story. * *An old man was walking along the beach and saw a young boy picking up starfishes and throwing them back into the ocean. As they neared each other and smiled, the man asked the boy why he was throwing them in the water.*

The young boy replied, 'The sun is up and the tide is low. They will die on the beach.'

The man said, 'There are miles of starfish washed up on the shore. How could you possibly make a difference?

The boy contemplated what the man said, and bent down, picked up a starfish and threw it the ocean. He said, 'It just made a difference for that one.'"

"Oh, I heard this story before," Marie says still looking puzzled. "How is it related to Faith and Trust?"

A couple from the beach walks into the restaurant and Rai and Stephanie wave hello.

"Well," says Stephanie, "You didn't hear our grandmother's spin on the tale. She said, '*Sometimes our dreams can feel overwhelming like a shore full of washed-up starfishes. We don't act because we don't believe following them will make a difference. We can choose to have the attitude like the old man who sees it as impossible or like the young boy who followed his heart to save as many as he could. He didn't know if throwing them back would save their lives. He trusted the ocean would do its job.*'"

Stephanie pauses to take a bite of her lunch and Rai continues the conversation.

"Marie, you may not always know what to do next, but you're never alone when you pursue your dreams. The Divine Spirit journeys along with you, whispering guidance that aligns you with the next steps, resources and people necessary to make your dreams happen.

Our grandmother called us the Gemini stars in her life. You can become a star of hope shining in others' lives too. More importantly, you can *star in your own life, when you let your Magical Essence radiate from your heart.*

Let go of control, confusion and simply learn to trust. *Letting go is the hardest part.* You take baby steps in building your Faith and stepping out in Trust."

Marie makes a confession: "I always wanted to be a famous jewelry designer. Over the years, I secretly stashed away dozens of sketchbooks filled with my designs." A smile comes over her face.

Stephanie and Rai hear the passion and excitement in her voice as she talks.

Smiling at Marie, Barb says "I told you for years, your creations are wonderful."

"I shared my dream with my parents," Marie states, looking down. "They told me I was silly and stupid. They said I couldn't make a decent living at designing jewelry. Didn't I ever hear the phrase 'starving artist?' They told me to get my head out of the clouds and grow up. I gave up on it, afraid to share it with anybody."

"You didn't give up on it completely," Stephanie says.

"I guess you're right," Marie replies. "I couldn't bear others rejecting my dreams. I kept it to myself holding onto a tiny glimmer of hope. Here I am today enjoying your dream. A dream that's literally up in the trees. I can see the possibilities if you don't give up. This is the vision I wrote down in the Ocean of Possibilities Guidebook.

If I understand you correctly, all I need to do is believe in my dream, have faith it's already mine, and trust the inspired action comes to me directly from the Divine Spirit, and it will happen? It just sounds too simple."

Stephanie and Rai smile and laugh. "Yep," they say together. And Rai adds, "Well, there is one more thing. You must be patient, have fun and stay relaxed with the process. The fun part is critical because it keeps your heart and mind open. Remember, the results don't always happen overnight.

We humans want to complicate everything. If you let go and trust, you'll achieve what you want with less effort. Solutions and opportunities will present themselves."

"Speaking of fun," Stephanie says rising from her seat, "Ready to go zip lining or take one of the eco-tours?"

Barb rises too and yells, "You know I love zip lining."

"What do think, Marie? What would you like to do?" Captain T asks.

"I'm in for zip lining," says Marie. "And it looks like a lot of fun exploring the forest up in the canopy too."

"Let's get going," the twins say in unison.

After a day of fun and laughter, the Captain, Barb and Marie walk to their treehouses to get ready for dinner.

The treehouses maximize luxurious relaxation with silk sheets and lavender handmade soaps. Marie enjoys the fresh air while resting in the hammock on her balcony. Her private treehouse overlooks the winding creek.

She enjoys a spa shower, dries off and wraps herself in a plush Turkish cotton robe. She puts on the teal sundress Barb gave her that morning, grabs the shawl and heads back down to the beach.

When she arrives, she removes her teal sandals, walking barefoot through the sand to join Barb and her father at their table. Digging her toes into the cool sand, she looks up and notices the gorgeous night with more stars than she's ever witnessed before.

After a day of outdoor adventures, a delicious dinner and a couple glasses of wine, an exhausted Marie decides to call it a night early. She runs into Stephanie and Rai as she walks across the lobby on her way to her treehouse. Marie says, "This place is awesome. I really enjoyed myself today. Thank you."

"You're welcome," reply the twins. "We have something for you."

Rai places a small, starfish in the palm of her hand. "Remember when fear takes over, in your mind's eye, see the star shining the way to your inner guidance, the connection to the Divine Spirit."

"Thanks, Rai."

Stephanie hands her a small rectangular box and says, "There are stars above us in the heavens and below us in the oceans, to remind us of the abundance the Divine Spirit wants to give us."

Marie opens the box and inside is a plaque with the quote: "Everything you want is waiting for you on the side of trust." A note card with three Faith and Trust affirmations is also included.

The sisters hug her and say they will see her in the morning.

When she gets back to the treehouse and readies herself for bed, Marie adds the three affirmations to the scroll:

- I trust the intelligence within me
- I allow myself to be guided by my intuition
- I freely express who I am

Slipping under the silky sheets, the cool, soft, smoothness feels like heaven against her skin. She thinks *'could it really be that simple?'* As she continues to reflect upon what these sisters accomplished, she begins to believe her dream can happen too. For the first time in her adult life, Marie *allows* herself to drift off envisioning the joy on the faces of the people who appreciate her artistic creations.

―⁂―

Wow you made it this far. Another item on your treasure hunt awaits you. You'll find it at www.annrusnak.com/intuition

*The Starfish Story: Adapted from "The Star Thrower" is part of a 16-page essay of the same name by Loren Eiseley.

CHAPTER 12

The Dreaded Pirates, Doubt and Fear

Marie awakens at 2:00 am. She thinks, *"The sisters made everything sound so simple. Maybe this faith and trust stuff works for them, but I'm not sure it will work for me."*

Questions swirl in Marie's mind and she can't fall back to sleep. She decides to get out of bed. She turns on the nightstand light and sees the starfish Rai gave her. She leaves her room to go to the lobby to make herself a cup of chamomile tea. Maybe the short walk in the evening air will help her sleep better.

She reaches the lobby and goes over to the beverage station to make herself a cup of tea. Instead of heading back to her treehouse, she sits on the sofa by the picture window looking out toward the beach.

A full moon has risen and its reflection dances on the gentle waves. She is so deep in thought, she doesn't hear Stephanie walk in. She startles Marie when she asks, "Mind if I join you?"

"Yes, please do," Marie answers.

"I didn't mean to scare you," Stephanie says as she joins Marie on the sofa and makes herself comfortable.

"It's okay, at least I wasn't holding my tea," she laughs.

Stephanie continues the conversation, "Something told me to come down here. It seemed urgent."

"Really?" Marie asked puzzled. "Your intuition told you to come down to the lobby?"

"Yes, my past experiences have taught me to trust and follow it."

"I want to learn more about Faith and Trust, Stephanie. I couldn't fall back to sleep because of the questions I have about following my inner voice," Marie says.

Stephanie responds with, "That's probably why I felt guided to come down here. Ask away."

"I look around at what you and Rai accomplished by following your guidance and I think to myself, *'there is no way I could do that.'* It's so *huge*."

"You're right, Marie," Stephanie replies.

Marie looks at her with a surprised expression on her face. She half expected Stephanie to argue with her and give her all the reasons why she *could* do it.

Stephanie continues, "There was a time in my life too, Marie, that I couldn't imagine doing everything by inspired action. *I was such a control freak.*

"Think of faith as a bridge over a foggy, misty crevice connecting you from where you are now to where you want to go.

Your dreams, the life you envision, and your destiny awaits you on the other side. You just need to cross that bridge. You don't know the width of the crevice, the condition of the bridge, and who you may encounter along the way. You can only see the first few inches of the bridge. This is where trust comes in. If you let fear take over, you'll never trust you can cross the bridge."

Marie brings her cup to her lips but never sips, as she is intrigued by Stephanie's metaphor.

"Look, Marie, you're just beginning this new journey. You need to start with baby steps, with the small things, when learning to following your inner guidance, your own Magical Essence. Pay attention to what happens when you follow it and what happens when you don't. The more you do it, the easier it will become.

Letting go is critical. Trust is faith in action."

Marie's eyes glance up toward the ceiling, taking a deep breath and letting it go, she returns Stephanie's gaze and says, "I don't know... It sounds scary to me."

As she sets her cup down on the coffee table, Stephanie's responds with, "I'm not saying you won't feel scared, but Fear and Doubt destroy dreams if you let them. They feed on uncertainty and will ultimately rob you of your potential, your destiny. They will keep you playing *small*.

Letting go and trusting goes against what the world teaches us, Marie. Your logical side uses your past experiences and current beliefs to help you make decisions to determine your actions, behaviors and habits.

When you feel scared and give in, you'll make decisions and take actions based on past experiences and that *fear* will, pulls you away from your dreams. Your biggest weapon against those dream stealers is Faith and Trust.

When you live your life this way, you can let go of control and take inspired action, even if it doesn't make sense at the time. Doors open for you and the way will be cleared. The Divine Spirit is always with you, taking care of you, keeping you safe and guiding the way."

"You make it sound so incredible, living this Pollyanna life," Marie says.

Stephanie replies, "You'll experience problems along the way and you can't ignore them. You'll be open to see things differently, even how the obstacles will show you a *better* way. I'm not talking about a problem-free existence. But when you live from a place of Faith and Trust, you become empowered to see what is and what isn't. Making life easier, a lot less stressful and an inner peace comes over you."

"Thanks," Marie replies. "You did a great job answering my questions."

Marie notices the dawning of the new day coming over the horizon.

"Oh my gosh, we're going to be on our way soon. I better get back to my room, change and pack up. Sorry I kept you up most of the night," Marie apologizes to Stephanie.

"No apology necessary. Here is an idea Rai shared with me and I found it helpful and maybe you will too. Start a Trust List."

"A list?"

"Yes, start a list of things you trust, like the sun rising every morning, or your next breath. Your friendship with Barb."

Marie interrupts, "Or my daughter's love, the fact I know I'm a child of the Universe, and that the seasons will come."

"You got the idea, Marie," Stephanie says smiling. "Every time you think of something, add it your list."

"I bet when I open my Guidebook, I'll find a 'Trust List' section," Marie says with a big grin.

Stephanie smiles back.

After a quick breakfast, the twins take their guest to the dock.

Marie hugs Stephanie and Rai and expresses her gratitude for a wonderful time. The sisters share words of wisdom with her before she boards:

"It's scary and unsettling when you're learning to step up to the next level in life. Remember: Faith and Trust cannot work for you unless you let go of control, let go of fear and take action. Take solace in the fact that up to this point, you have survived everything that has happened in your life. You'll learn to find comfort in the uncertainty."

From the boat, Marie waves goodbye to the twins, holding the starfish in her hand.

The Captain and Barb join her. Marie continues looking at the sisters until she can no longer see them on the horizon. Captain T announces they will soon arrive at the Island of Self-Empowerment.

"Wow, that sounds so exciting!" Marie exclaims. Then, she suddenly realizes only one island remains and a sadness comes over her. Part of her doesn't want the journey to end.

She puts the starfish in her shorts pocket, grabs her Guidebook and sits on the deck lounge chair, where she creates her Trust List. Before she knows it, she wrote three pages.

Surprisingly, while she writes her list, she finds that she is doubting herself more and more. She thinks to herself, *"Stephanie and Rai didn't worry about taking care of a child, like I do. How am I supposed to start a business on my own? Maybe if I was younger or my marriage was more secure, I could. Heck! I'm still trying to decide what to do about Lloyd. This isn't the time to be frivolous."*

Marie looks up and sees the sun begin to disappear behind a cloud of black smoke.

The Magical Essence sails closer to the smoke and a large, fiery burning heap blocks the way. Marie observes how the heap appears endless with no way around it.

"Only one more island," she thinks to herself. And of course, this would happen. Why does this always seem to happen when I'm so close to achieving something important?" Marie says aloud in a tone of despair.

She kneels on the deck, sobbing. "So close and once again my dreams are yanked from me," Marie does not realize Barb and Captain T are also on the deck looking at the burning blockade.

A sudden roar catches everyone's attention. Rising from the water they see a huge menacing figure emerging from the red and black smoke. It looks like a muscular man with a large club in one of his hands. She feels a deep sense of Fear in his presence. His deep brow forms into a scowl looking down at her. Fear overtakes Marie, making her feel like a helpless child.

He growls at Marie, warning her not to go any further. He bellows, "I will spare your life if you turn over your treasure now!"

Another figure rises out of the ocean, just as menacing. She is filled with Doubt as he yells at her, "You talk about living your dreams. Do you really think holding onto your inner treasure will make it happen? You're in fantasy land. What will happen when you return to reality tomorrow? Give us your treasure and turn this boat around!"

Filled with both Fear and Doubt, Marie collapses onto the deck and places her head into her hands. Between her sobs she shouts, "They are right. This is all fantasy and not the *real* world. If I divorce Lloyd, I will need to pay bills, find a job and a place to live. I have responsibilities with Elizabeth."

Marie continues, "I can't do this. Turning around is so much easier, safer. But I don't want to surrender my treasure. Not when I just found it," she screams. "This is so much bigger than me. I can't do this. I won't make it," Marie says between sobs.

Captain T walks over to her and offers his hand, helping her to her feet.

"I'm here and we can get through this together. You are not alone. You're *never* alone. Remember what Stephanie and Rai said about the Divine Spirit. It is always with you. It's time to turn around and face your fears."

Marie turns around and Captain T places his hand on her left shoulder. He instructs her to quiet herself to feel the Divine Spirit within, guiding her.

She closes her eyes and takes a few slow, deep breaths and starts feeling herself calm down. She feels a warm glow on her shoulder. Something tells her to focus on the outcome of her vision. She imagines starting a new life with positive people around her. She decides that her God-given dreams are bigger than the Pirates, which filled her with Fear and Doubt.

She hears an echo that sounds like the Captain's voice, even though she knows he's standing right next to her, "Focus on your vision and let go."

Barb comes over and places her hand on Marie's other shoulder.

The twins' words fill her mind. *"Faith and Trust always defeat Fear and Doubt. Open your heart to let Faith and Trust in."*

With her eyes still closed, she remembers the starfish in her pocket, pulls it out and envisions it's light shining the way to the fulfillment of her dreams. She feels the warmth of love surrounding her. She hears whispers, "Fear and Doubt can't harm you. The Divine Spirit is with you, protecting you with His love."

The calmness clears her mind. She says, "This isn't just about Elizabeth, it's about me too. Thinking we can stay with Lloyd and ignore his mental abuse is the *real* fantasy. I heard someone once say, 'you can't *un-ring* a bell' because once it's in your brain, it's difficult to remove.

"If I stay and put up with his undermining remarks, Elizabeth will normalize this sort of behavior as acceptable. For the sake of her self-worth, I must leave him. The best gift I can give her is a strong sense of self-worth."

Marie continues, "While I'm sure he'll want visitation rights, I can feel assured she'll spend most of her time in a safe, supportive and nurturing environment. She can learn to stick up for herself and counter negativity by seeing how I handle it. I will be her mentor."

Opening her eyes, she looks at the Captain and Barb and tells them, "Since he's unwilling to change his behavior, I've made up my mind. I'm leaving Lloyd. My daughter's self-worth depends on it. So, does mine. Let's find a way to get through this blockade!"

Placing her hand on her hips, in a gesture of defiance, she turns to face the obstacle. She isn't sure if the sailboat will make it. She decides to take the chance and Trust. She feels a connection to God and her thoughts focus on how everything is possible with Him.

She takes a deep breath and lets go of the Fear and Doubt about her new life. She concludes she doesn't need to worry about *how* it will happen, because that job belongs to the Divine Spirit. After all, God gave her the dreams. She trusts He will make them happen if she takes inspired action.

The departing words of the sisters' echo in her mind, *"Up to this point, you have survived everything that has happened in your life. Learn to find comfort in the uncertainty."*

Something inside tells her to close her eyes again and shout out, "I will not let uncertainty hold me back." She opens her eyes to sees the blockade evaporating, revealing a small boat with two men dressed like pirates.

Captain T says, "Meet the pirates Ian Fear and his cousin Jonathan Doubt."

Ian is handsome. His strong chiseled jaw line and brown, almond-shaped eyes give him a sexy, steamy look. His brown hair sports a touch of gray at the temples.

His cousin Jonathan's dreamy appearance comes from his wavy blondish brown mane and silvery blue eyes. His broad shoulders and dazzling smile adds an alluring, seductive quality.

Fear and Doubt weren't as bad as she imagined. Their familiarity catches her off-guard. It is as if she has known them most of her life, like childhood friends. She wonders why these two good-looking men would go around terrorizing people.

Ian and Jonathan take their hats off and bow their heads in a gentlemanly manor during introductions. They state, "It's a pleasure to finally meet you in person, Marie. Until now, we've been a big part of your life, so don't think you can simply dismiss us. We have no intention of leaving you alone. We'll show up again, bringing more of our family for reinforcement.

"After all, we're pirates and it's our job to steal, loot and plunder treasures of the heart."

Marie notices they have no hold on her now. She thinks, *"It's really that simple. I shift my thinking and take action to clear the blocks Fear and Doubt create."*

Something instantly transforms in Marie and she feels *free*. She smiles at the cousins and says, "I'm sure you'll catch me off guard in days to come. Now I know what you look like and I'm no longer scared or seduced by you. I know I'm not alone when it comes to dealing with you. The Divine Spirit protects me."

Ian and Jonathan get angry, pull up anchor and sail away. Marie can see the Island of Self-Empowerment in front of them, from the deck of the Magical Essence. She's ready to launch her dreams and discover her unstoppable success.

CHAPTER 13

Step 7 - Island of Self-Empowerment

Marie takes a deep breath and lets it out slowly as the two pirates sail away. She turns around and puts her arms around Barb and the Captain.

"Thank you so much. I knew you stood with me and the feeling of love filled and surrounded me. For the first time, I knew, what to do and a feeling of inner peace moved into my heart," Marie says.

Barb giggles and says, "Would the word 'empower' describe your feelings?"

Marie starts laughing and says, "Gee, I guess that's why the Island of Self-Empowerment is right in front of us!"

A smile stretches across Captain T's face and he nods slightly and says, "Ah Marie, you reconnected to the divine within, to your unique, authentic self. That is your Magical Essence (ME). Welcome back."

The sailboat pulls into the harbor and docks at the marina. Barb, Captain T and Marie walk toward the clubhouse to join a slim, golden-haired athletic-built woman holding a picnic basket and waving to them with her other hand.

Captain T introduces Laura to Marie. Marie shakes her hand and remarks how the aqua sundress compliments her beautiful blue eyes and curly golden hair.

"Come Marie, I planned a picnic for us. We'll catch up with you two later," she says to Barb and her father with a wink.

Marie sees a private picnic area with a spread-out vibrant blanket awaiting them. She lays out the items Laura hands her from the basket.

Laura begins the conversation, "You experienced quite a journey to get here, didn't you?"

"Yes," Marie replies. "What a journey! I finally learned to appreciate my value as a person. It feels a little strange saying it and believing it at the same time."

Laura responds, "Now, I am here to help you. You may notice your treasure chest contains, silver, gems and pearls but no gold. Any treasure chest of great value contains gold. Gold holds a special place in history and human development. This rare sun yellow metal is the only metal that will not tarnish or rust.

Gold's value appreciates over time...It can be saved and retrieved much later with predictability of its value. If you want gold in your treasure chest, you must put it there. That's because you must acquire them by using your gifts. Golf doubloons represent the value you bring to the world."

A huge grin appears on Marie's face and she snickers to herself, thinking how Lloyd always told her about Gold being a wise investment. She notices Laura's perplexed look and waves her hand in a "never mind" motion.

"It's just something my husband said about gold. It's not important, please continue Laura."

"When talking about self-empowerment, I want to caution you about potentially confusing the words '*worth*' and '*value.*' They *don't* mean the same thing."

"What do you mean?" Marie asks, then continues to enjoy the scrumptious sandwich Laura had prepared for her.

"According to the dictionary, **'worth' is:** *The quality of a person that lends importance, value and merit.* As a creation of God, you come into this world with self-worth. No one can take it away... although you might not see it in yourself.

'Value' is different. It is: *That which is rendered desirable or useful... highly regarded.*

Developing and sharing your treasures to enhance the lives around you adds value to what you do. There are many ways you add significance to others' lives for the better: such as using your talents, by encouraging others, and by being there for somebody else.

I share this quote with all my clients. It was said by Steve Bow, a corporate executive I know:

'God's gift to us is more talent and ability than we'll ever hope to use in our lifetime. Our gift to God is to develop as much of that talent and ability as we can in this lifetime.'"

Marie asks, "What if you're not sure of your talents or gifts which bring value?"

Laura smiles and states enthusiastically, "That's a big reason I became a personal empowerment coach!

"You see, Marie, it's not always easy to see those things in ourselves. Not seeing or recognizing your talent can cause frustration in trying to live a life of purpose. This leaves you feeling stuck because you can't move forward no matter what you do."

Laura shifts on the blanket to make herself more comfortable before continuing.

"As a coach, I help people identify and remove the blocks that keep them stuck. I teach them how to empower themselves with confidence to use their God-given potential to make a positive change in the world by living their dreams *on their terms.*

My life wasn't much different than yours, Marie. I came from an abusive home. I dreamed of being wealthy. I was put down and belittled because of that dream. I was told wealthy people were evil and did bad things to get their money. My parents made sure I understood pursuing my dream would send me to hell."

Marie interrupts, "Wow! That IS my story!"

"You're not alone. Many of us have some story around money. I learned the truth about the neutrality of money. If you decide to answer your entrepreneurial calling, eventually you'll need to deal with your negative money stories. Business is about money. Symptoms of deeper negative beliefs show up as money issues. Empowering people to move forward, to live their dreams once we remove those beliefs, motivates me."

"What a great calling," Marie replies as she adjusts into a more comfortable position on the blanket, "helping others believe in themselves so they can achieve their dreams."

The two continue to talk, sharing their stories, when Marie notices parasailing in the sky just off the coast.

"I've always wanted to do that," Marie says standing up to get a better view.

"Let's go," says Laura. "I know the owner of Larry's Parasailing Adventures. He's a client of mine. One of the ways I help my clients face fear is to encourage them to do something *scary*. Parasailing is the perfect way to let go and look at the beauty around you. Are you ready for your first parasailing adventure?"

Marie responds immediately with an enthusiastic, "Yes!"

They pack up the picnic and head over to Larry's Parasailing Adventures. Laura suggest Marie join her for a tandem parasailing experience to enjoy the fun together. As the boat speeds off, and they are lifted up into the air, an awestruck Marie sees dolphins and rays in the translucent waters below.

"I can't believe this feeling of freedom!" Marie shouts to be heard over the wind and boat motor.

Laura responds, "You can always feel like this if you choose. Especially when you let go of fear."

Looking over at Laura, Marie points to a group of people setting up a stage and chairs and says, "Looks like some kind of celebration will happen tonight. I hope we can attend."

"We can do whatever you want. Never forget this is *your* journey."

"Can't wait," says Marie.

Their ride through the sky comes to an end and as they return to the dock, Marie shouts, "What an exhilarating flight!"

"Glad you enjoyed it," Laura replies.

They walk along the beach to return to the clubhouse when Marie says, "Oh my! Look at all the sand dollars."

Laura explains, "Yes, they often wash up on the shore. I think of them as a sign of prosperity coming my way."

"What a wonderful thought," Marie says while picking up a few to use in her jewelry designs.

They reach the clubhouse to find Captain T and Barb returning. "Perfect timing," says Captain T. "Laura and I must attend to a few details before night fall."

Barb and Marie rent a couple of scooters to explore the town. A shell store beckons Marie to visit. "Do you mind if we go in?" she asks Barb.

"Lead the way. This is one of my favorite shops."

The large selection thrills Marie. She acts like a kid in a candy shop. Earlier, she sketched several ideas for her 'Ocean of Possibilities Jewelry' line in the "Thoughts Section" of her Guidebook. Marie picks up items to make a necklace and a matching bracelet she envisioned.

The shop also sells sand dollars and starfish prepped and ready to use. Marie adds a large variety of gold and silver metal shells to her basket. Near the checkout counter she notices several types of journals and feels guided to purchase a few.

They finish their shopping and Marie tells Barb she wants to head back to the Magical Essence to rest.

Feeling refreshed after a 20-minute nap, Marie, takes the scalloped shell Regina gave her and using the drill she picked up at the craft store, she carefully drills a tiny hole on each side. She attaches a small sand dollar on each side of the shell. Next, she glues a tiny cluster of red, green, blue, yellow and white crystals to the upper left corner to represent the jewels in her chest.

She twists thin strands of gold and silver cording and strings alternating beads of gold and silver between pearls on each side of the sand dollars. She opts to do the beads half way on each side and attaches the starfish clasp at the end.

She finishes her creation by delicately painting a very thin gold line in the shell's grooves. Using smaller versions of the shells, she creates a matching bracelet.

She also uses the silver and gold metal sand dollars to make a necklace for Barb. Marie twists a leather band together and attaches it to a silver boat wheel, producing a bracelet for Captain T.

Marie notices the sun setting in the sky and expects Barb and her father will be back soon. She jumps in the shower. Then as she dresses, Barb knocks on her door.

"You up?" she calls.

Marie opens the door and Barb remarks about how beautiful she looks. "You're glowing! There is such a peaceful look about you," she comments to Marie.

Seeing the necklace, Marie is wearing, Barb continues, "Oh my gosh, I love what you did with the shell. The necklace is gorgeous. I guess you didn't rest for very long."

"You're right, I'm too excited! And, I have a surprise for you." Marie says presenting Barb with the sand dollar necklace.

She gasps and says, "This is very *beautiful*. Thank you so much. Guess what? I have a big surprise for you too. Come up on the deck."

They walk upstairs together and Marie sees Laura and Captain T waiting. They comment on how beautiful she looks. Marie notices how comfortable see feels accepting the compliments.

"Looks like connecting to your authentic self agrees with you," Captain T says emphatically.

They walk toward the dock and Laura points to her car. Barb and Marie get in the backseat. Barb says, "I need to blindfold you. We wouldn't want to ruin your surprise."

While Barb ties on the blindfold, Marie ask, "I noticed a festival being set up while parasailing this afternoon. Do you think we can attend it later?"

"Sure, we can," replies Barb.

Within a few minutes they reach their destination. Barb helps Marie out of the car. Captain T removes the blindfold and Marie opens her eyes to see a banner draped across the road. Her mouth drops wide open as she reads:

"Welcome, Marie, to the Celebrate YOU Now™ Festival."

She looks around and suddenly realizes the festival is *specifically* for her. She finds herself speechless when a band plays "Welcome Marie!"

She puts her hand up to her mouth to cover the look of shock she is feeling from seeing hundreds of people in attendance, looking at her and clapping. She says, "I don't understand, why the big festival? What is the reason for this celebration?"

"Because *you* are worth celebrating, Marie," says Captain T. "When a soul is lost and rediscovers themselves, connecting back to the person they are meant to be, to live the life designed by their Creator, it's worth celebrating."

As they walk toward the square, Marie sees all her mentors along this journey coming at her with open arms: Regina, Paul, Judith, Marcus, DelaRose, Stephanie and Rai.

The evening is a huge success of heart-lifting island music, tropical food and delicious drinks. When the festivities come to a close, Marie exclaims to all her mentors, "How can I ever repay you for all you've done for me?"

"Just stay true to yourself and follow your dreams," they say. "That is the best payment we can receive."

"I'm going to miss you so much," Marie says with tears welling in her eyes.

Laura replies, "Remember, the Divine Spirit connects all of us. All you need to do is quiet your mind, go within and you'll locate us there. We're always with you, ready to guide you if you ask, believe, and take inspired action."

The party winds down and the guest begin to depart. Marie request to walk back to the boat alone. She wants some time to reflect on the day's events.

"Of course," Barb says as she and her father get into Laura's car. "Enjoy your walk. We'll see you back at the boat."

As she takes a stroll down the beach, Marie realizes for the first time what it truly feels like to be loved and appreciated by the people in her life. Finally, she discovered how to surround herself with supportive, positive people who believe in her.

CHAPTER 14

God's Sake, Follow Your Heart

Following a candlelight trail to the Marina, Marie realizes how much this journey changed her life. She knows she'll never again be the same person, nor would she want to be. A lot of uncertainty lies ahead, but she feels confident she can handle anything that will come her way.

Marie knows her faith will grow stronger with each step she takes in Trust. She reaches the park where she and Laura enjoyed lunch earlier. She notices a young woman with soft wavy brown hair, sitting on a bench crying.

"Are you alright?" she asks.

The young woman looks up and responds, "Oh, you're Marie, the guest of honor tonight. I'm embarrassed to say this but I feel so lost. I wish I felt confident like you. You're so self-assured."

"Well, I don't know about that," Marie says. "Just a few days ago, I felt lost too. I needed to make a difficult decision about leaving an unhappy marriage for the sake of my daughter.

Although I decided to leave, it will require me to take uncomfortable steps at first, but that's how I'll begin to live a rich, fulfilling life. I place my trust in the Divine Spirit to guide me on the next steps to take."

"See this necklace?" Marie asks, motioning her hand around her neck.

"Yes," replies the young woman. "I also see it matches your beautiful bracelet."

"Yes, it does." Marie says with a smile.

"We come into this world unstoppable, with an inner treasure, which is filled with everything necessary to live a happy, prosperous and successful life. Growing up we get lost and lose sight of our worth and the wonderful life we're meant to live.

I created this necklace to remind me of the seven steps I took on this journey." Marie pauses for a moment before continuing. "The journey to ME to rediscover my treasure chest of worthiness."

Marie points to the scallop shell and continues her story. "The first step on my journey, or any journey including yours, begins with **Hope**. But, if you don't take responsibility for your thoughts, actions and outcomes, then hope turns into hopeless wishes."

"The second step is **Responsibility**. Taking responsibility empowers me to continue forward on this adventure." Her fingers touch the twisted strands of cording. "These strands represent responsibility. Without them, the creation of the necklace would not be possible. This piece of jewelry is the first in my new 'Ocean of Possibilities' collection."

Marie now points to one of the silver beads. She explains to the young woman the bead, represents the self-love in the third step, **Forgiveness**. "I can forgive myself and begin to love myself unconditionally. I learned mistakes are a part of life's process and, not a life sentence to stay stuck in a prison of the past."

Pointing to the tiny cluster of colored crystals on the shell, Marie continues. "Making mistakes gives me the freedom to polish and shape the gems of my self-confidence. I can confidently develop my natural abilities, my talents and gifts, and stay connected to Universal Source, through the fourth step of **Gratitude**."

Marie moves her finger to one of the pearl beads and says, "These beads represent the pearls of self-esteem in my treasure chest. This brings us to step five, **Courage**. It takes courage for me to think highly of myself, to stay open to making necessary changes, to step outside my comfort zone and boldly step into the person I'm meant to be.

"Courage allows me to take the sixth step, **Faith** and **Trust**."

Marie unclasps the necklace, removes it from her neck and holds the crystal-studded starfish clasp between her finger and thumb.

She continues her story, "This starfish reminds me we live in an abundant world. All I need to do is let go of control and the 'how to' of obtaining my dream, by recognizing the Divine Spirit will always provide for us.

This step enables me to defeat Fear and Doubt, allowing me to close this journey with the seventh step, **Self-Empowerment.**"

Marie clasps the necklace around her neck again before continuing.

Pointing to a gold bead, Marie says, "Now I'm empowered to use my talents to add value to other people's lives, which brings gold into my treasure, opening the possibilities to a rich, prosperous life," she concludes tapping on one of the sand dollars.

"Thanks for sharing your story," the woman says with sincere gratitude.

"You're welcome," Marie says, "Would you do me a favor?"

"Yes," the young woman replies.

"First, please tell me your name?"

A big smile brightens the young woman's face and she says, "Melissa, my name is Melissa."

"Glad to meet you Melissa. Will you hold your arm straight out?" Marie requests.

With a curious look on her face, Melissa extends her arm.

Marie removes the bracelet from her arm and puts it around Melissa's wrist. She closes the clasp saying, "I'm empowered to pursue my childhood dream to design jewelry. This is one of the pieces I made since making the decision to pursue my dream. I'm honored to give this gift to you. The favor I am asking is if you will accept my gift?"

Melissa says, "Thank you. I don't know what to say. You're too generous."

"I learned on this journey, when you give, you also open yourself up to receiving from the Universe. Please accept this bracelet given with love." Marie says exuberantly. You are the perfect recipient for this piece of jewelry. Please enjoy it."

Marie says goodbye and continues walking back to the boat. She feels tired, yet fulfilled from all the excitement and celebration. She greets Barb and Captain T with her gratitude and shares how much she enjoyed herself. Then she explains, that if she doesn't go to bed, she will probably drop from exhaustion.

She retires to her cabin. But before giving in to sleep, she opens her treasure chest to remove the scroll and notices several new pieces of gold.

Curious, she opens the guidebook and sees the final tab which reads "Adding Gold Doubloons." The title page states "Gold Doubloons – Adding Value to Life," with a quote underneath by Leo Buscaglia,

"Your talent is God's gift to you; What you do with it is your gift to God."
She reads the instructions under the quote:

1. God gives us desires and dreams to bring as gifts to exchange with the world.
2. We are here to contribute something of value to others.
3. Use the questions in the section to discover ways to use your talents
4. Write down the first thoughts that enter your mind. Don't spend time analyzing the questions and your answers.

A smile comes over her face. Marie looks forward to completing this section tomorrow. She finishes her evening ritual, changes into her night shirt, crawls under the covers, falling asleep immediately.

Marie sleeps peacefully and awakens refreshed and excited about the days ahead. She dresses and heads to the deck in time to see the sun rising.

Barb joins her on the deck and one of the crew members asks what they would like for breakfast. After giving their selections, Marie looks out to the dock and notices Laura walking toward the ship. She waves to her. Laura comes boards holding a card in her hand.

"Would you care to join us for breakfast, Laura?" Barb asks.

"Yes, thank you," she says.

"I'm glad to see you before we leave," Marie says. "Thank you, again, for the beautiful party last night."

"You're welcome. I realized this morning I forgot to give you the last three affirmations," Laura says handing the card to Marie.

Marie reads them.
- I love myself totally in the NOW
- I have unlimited potential
- I am a YES! person

"Thank you, Laura."

"My pleasure. Did you open your Guidebook yet?" Laura asks.

"Yes, I noticed the final section: 'Adding Gold Doubloons.'" Marie says.

"Good, let your inner guidance direct you when answering the questions. They will help you get to know yourself better while you continue to become the self-fulfilled person you're destined to be.

I also recommend you revisit the false beliefs you wrote in the 'Thoughts Section.' Turn them into positive statements. Keeping a journal helped me, Marie. I took my new messages and turned them into a positive Personal Declaration about myself. I wrote the Declaration on the first page of the journal and read it every day."

"What a great idea," Marie says. "Good thing I purchased a few journals yesterday."

A lively conversation ensues among the three when Captain T makes his appearance and joins them.

"Good morning, everyone," Captain T says cheerfully.

Laura confesses, "I hate to say good-bye, but I know you're getting ready to take off. Marie, it was a pleasure meeting you. I enjoyed parasailing together."

"Me too," says Marie smiling.

She hugs Laura and then waves to her as the boat departs from the dock. Soon the island disappears below the horizon.

Barb notices a woeful expression on Marie's face and asks, "Are you alright?"

"Yes, I'm fine. Sad our trip is coming to an end."

"I know what you mean," Barb replies.

"When will we get back?"

"Around lunch time," Barb says.

"What!?" A surprised Marie says. "That soon? I thought it would take a couple of days to get back"

"Not in a magical ocean. Your trip in the Ocean of Possibilities lasts as long as you need," Barb answers. "As humans, we are destined to grow and, when it is time to transform to another level of development, we will return to sail the Ocean of Possibilities."

Marie remarks, "I guess I better go pack my things and get the gift I made for your father."

"When you're done packing, he would like you to stop by his cabin," Barb states.

Marie walks down the hallway to the Captain's room. She notices the door is half-open. When she reads the name plate on the door, *Tirips Enivid*, she shakes her head and says to herself, *"I forgot to ask him what it means."*

When she knocks on the door she notices the name plate's reflection in the mirror across the room. Feeling weak in her knees, she puts her hand over her heart as she reads it in the reflection:

"divinE spiriT"

Captain T sees her and holds her steady as they walk over to the table. Marie collapses into the chair, shaking. He brings her a glass of water, but she can barely hold it in her trembling hands. He sits in the chair next to her, softly smiling while he lets her gather herself.

The room radiates with love. She feels so much warmth in her heart that it feels like it could burst open. She reaches over and hugs Him and He hugs her back.

She lets go of His embrace and says, "Why me? Why did you select me for this journey? Does Barb know? Of course, Barb knows. Wait, if you're the Divine Spirit, who is Barb?"

Marie pauses long enough from her questions to allow the Captain to answer.

"I've been trying to get your attention for *years*, Marie. I'm here to answer your prayers. I send people into your life to help you receive those answers. I do this for *all* my children. You are a **M**agnificent **E**xpression of the Universe, my daughter."

Marie whispers, "No wonder Barb feels like a Godsend to me. She is."

"I'm always sending invitations to my children, to let them know life needn't be so difficult. It's time to let go of the struggling, stress, worry, and anxiety. People don't always accept my invitation to come back to their true selves." Captain T says. "You've been an excellent student."

He notices the gift on the table and asks Marie, "For me?"

"Yes," she says handing it to Him. He opens it and sees a gold ship's wheel attached with gold cording twisted in the leather straps.

"I love the bracelet," He says putting it on. "It gives me pleasure to see you giving back by using your talents. This trip will come to an end soon and you'll go back into your world. I want to share some departing wisdom with you before you go."

"Yes, Captain," says Marie. "For God's sake, please do."

They both laugh.

CHAPTER 15

A New Legacy Begins

Marie rises from the chair feeling steadier now.

"Remember I'm always with you," the Captain starts. "It's important to surround yourself with supportive people who *believe in you*. The inner peace you feel, the connection to your authentic self is new. Protect it. You'll continue to let go of habits and behaviors that once supported your old self and form new ones to support your new beliefs. Soon these new feelings will become second nature to you.

There will be people who won't be happy with the changes you've made in yourself and your life. They won't know how to react or fit in. That's okay. At times, you will need to let go of people and activities to make room for where you are headed on your journey. The decision *always rests in your hands.*"

She looks at the Captain with an awestruck expression, taking in every word, He says into her heart.

He continues sharing Divine Wisdom, "As you sail through life, you can't always avoid the storms and rough waters; just move through them and keep on sailing. As I promised, I will be with you.

You're here to add value to your life, to add gold to your treasure and to contribute something to the world. Expect along the way you will again run into pirates who want to steal from you. Fear and Doubt warned you they will bring reinforcements from their family, such as worry, anxiety, stress, and discouragement…, just to name a few. With each new challenge you overcome, your Faith and Trust will grow stronger. Stay focused on your vision, follow your inner voice, take inspired action, and you will effortlessly sail through life.

Any questions or thoughts, Marie?"

"Captain," Marie inquires, "I keep hearing the words 'inspired action.' Can you tell me more?"

"Marie, you need to become still so you can hear your inner voice, your intuition. Your authentic self, your true ME (Magical Essence), is connected to the Divine within. Following your inner guidance goes against society's norm, but trust it and *act on it* even if the answers don't make sense."

Your Magical Essence is everything that uniquely makes you, YOU. You came into this world to use your essence to blossom into the fullest Magnificent Expression of your true nature. It is that part of you which is connected to the infinite capacity of unlimited possibilities.

"You can give to God and the world no greater service than to make the most of yourself."

Marie nods her head in acknowledgement.

He shares one last piece of advice with her, "Marie there are no mistakes, only learning experiences. Years from now you'll reflect and realize Lloyd is in your life as a gift from me. Beyond giving you a beautiful daughter, he opened your eyes to what you didn't want. Knowing what you don't want is as powerful as knowing what you do want. It motivates you to make positive changes in your life."

The Captain glances out the window and notices they are entering the harbor at Paradise Cove.

"Looks like we arrived," he said. "Now I have another gift for you."

"Another gift?" Marie says. "I am feeling very spoiled."

"As your Creator, I intend to give you many more gifts. Gifts just waiting for you to claim."

He takes her hand and turns it so her palm faces up. He places his compass in the center of her palm and folds her fingers over it. He says, "Use your Magical Essence to sail through life's adventures with self-empowerment as your directional wind. Let your thoughts navigate the maps of your dreams. Use this compass to know you're always on the right path. As long as, it's pointing to True ME, you won't get lost or go off course."

"Thank you so much," Marie says with tears of gratitude falling down her cheeks.

"Marie, it's important for you to continue your morning and evening transformation routine to enable your new positive beliefs to permanently take hold."

"I will, Captain, I promise," she answers.

The crew carries Barb and Marie's luggage to the oceanfront cottage as Barb, Marie and the Captain meet on the ship's deck.

Barb says to Marie, "I hope you don't mind, but I'm spending the next few weeks with you. How about we grab some lunch at Café Joes?"

"I'd like that very much. I could use the company over these next few weeks. Fear and Doubt will be lurking and your support will help with the transition time. Thanks Barb," Marie replies.

Everybody gathers on the dock to say their good-byes.

Marie gives the Captain a big hug and as she does, notices a 'Help Wanted' sign in a shop window behind him. A sudden overwhelming feeling rushes over her and she blurts aloud: "I want to stay here in Paradise Cove. This is where Elizabeth and I will begin our new lives. Captain, I love you so much."

"I love you too, Marie. Remember, I'm always here for you," the Captain replies as he steps on the boat. The engines power up and he lifts his hand to salute her. She sees he is wearing the bracelet she made him. The sun shining behind him creates a halo effect around his body. Marie returns his salute.

"Barb, would you mind if I check out the shop with the Help Wanted sign?"

"Of course not," Barb says. "I'll meet you at Café Joes. Take your time."

Marie practically flies up the dock to the shop. A bell announces her arrival as she enters the "Treasures on the Dock" shop.

She looks around and sees it contains 'treasure' from the local artists. An easel near the entrance displays a beautiful sign:

"The greatest gift one can give is to encourage others to see their potential."

"What a beautiful thought," she thinks. *"This would be a great place for me to display my jewelry line."*

The shop owner appears and asks if she needs any help. Marie points to the sign in the window and says, "I'm moving here and I'm inquiring about the job."

"Perfect. Tourist season is almost here. I'm Mrs. Caruthers."

"I'm Marie, it's a pleasure to meet you."

They exchange pleasantries and Mrs. Caruthers decides to hire Marie. She tells Marie the shop was a dream of hers because she always wanted a place where artists could display their works of art. The artists rent an area within the shop and Mrs. Caruthers keeps a small commission for selling their items.

"This is our third year. It's a favorite among the tourist and locals," she says. "Oh, by the way, call me Catherine. Where are you staying?"

"Right now, I'm staying with a friend while I look for a place for my daughter and me," Marie answers.

"I know the perfect place!" Catherine replies, "It's small, but I think it will work out well for you. Go to this address. I'll call Sarah to let her know you're on your way."

"Thanks, Catherine."

Marie looks out over the harbor, as she exits the store and notices the Magical Essence heading away from the dock and toward the horizon. She sees Barb waving to her from Café Joes and rushes over to share the good news with her about the job and her possible new home.

"I know Sarah," Barb says. "All her cottages are cute, well-kept and a short walk to the beach. Take your time checking it out. I'll wait here for you." Marie thinks to herself, *"Yes, Barb is a God-send. A guardian angel sent to watch over me."*

"Thanks, Barb," Marie says. "I feel Unstoppable and Fabulous!"

"I guess that makes you Unstopulous™!" Barb laughs.

Marie meets Sarah, who shows her a beautiful white-washed beach cottage and lets her know it will be ready in three weeks.

"Sarah, that works perfectly," Maire responds enthusiastically. "I'm picking my daughter up in a couple weeks. Right now, I'm staying with a friend." They finalize the arrangements and Sarah leaves l her sitting on the cottage's porch swing.

She closes her eyes, listening to the roar of the ocean in the distance. She thinks about how she will receive half the proceeds from the sale of her home. She receives an inspiration that she can also substitute teach to supplement her income, while building her jewelry empire. She trusts the Universe will provide if she takes inspired action.

A smile comes to her lips. "I can do this!" she says out loud.

She knows keeping her promise to herself won't be easy. She'll need to get through the divorce, deal with visitation rights, and the inevitable criticism from her parents. She realizes she can't isolate Elizabeth from all the negativity, but she can teach her how to keep it from affecting her. She now possesses the tools.

Marie opens her eyes and looks down at the wooden chest she purchased on her way out of the 'Treasures on the Dock' shop and smiles. She can't wait to tell her daughter about their new home and her new job. She thinks, *"Yes, I can give her the tools, the encouragement, share the lessons I learned and teach her how to connect to the Divine Spirit."*

Marie briefly reflects on the words from the first night of her journey… *'If you accept and complete the journey, you can follow your heart's desire, live life your way, going beyond your dreams. You will fulfill the promise for your daughter and create a new legacy for her and future generations.'*

She rises from the swing, glances at her compass and notices it still points to her true ME.

She begins walking to join Barb, when her phone rings. She looks down at the treasure chest in her hand as she says to Elizabeth, "Honey, do I have a story to tell you! I went on the journey of a lifetime. You and I are going to start a new life, full of adventure and fun. It's time to go on a treasure hunt to discover our buried treasures. You're going to love The Journey to ME!"

The final item to add to your "Unstoppable Success Kit" is at www.annrusnak.com/treasurehunt

MARIE'S 21 AFFIRMATIONS FOR UNSTOPPABLE SUCCESS

Treasure Chest – Self-worth

- I am good enough
- I love being me
- I am worth loving

Hope & Responsibility - Shell

- I rise above all limitations
- I have the power to make changes
- I create wonderful new beliefs for myself

Forgiveness - Silver

- I love and accept myself
- I treat myself with unconditional love
- I am perfect exactly as I am

Gratitude - Gems

- I am willing to see my own magnificence

- I think and speak positively
- I accept all parts of myself

Courage - Pearls

- This year I do the mental work for positive change
- I am my own unique self
- I am a natural winner

Faith & Trust - Starfish

- I trust the intelligence within me
- I allow myself to be guided by my intuition
- I freely express who I am

Self-Empowerment - Gold Doubloons

- I love myself totally in the NOW
- I have unlimited potential
- I am a YES! person

Would you like the same gift Marie received?

Receive your gift at **www.TheJourneytoMeGift.com.** That is where you can download your very own "Unstoppable Success Kit: A Simple and Easy Way to Attract Success in Less Than 5 Minutes A Day." Your Kit includes a motivational video, an inspirational audio and Anchor ME Playbook™ of the 21 affirmations given to Marie.

MARIE'S MORNING AND NIGHTLY TRANSFORMING ROUTINE

Read all affirmations with feeling and emotion.

Day One

 Evening: Write out and read the first three affirmations *(Treasure Chest – Self-worth set)*
 Fall asleep repeating the words, *"I choose to see my worthiness because I exist as a child of God."*

Day Two

 Morning: Read first three affirmations aloud.
 Evening: Write out the next three affirmations *(Hope - Responsibility)* along with previous affirmation. - total six.
 Read all six affirmations.
 Start writing your heart-felt vision.
 Fall asleep repeating the words, *"I choose to see my worthiness because I exist as a child of God."*

Day Three

 Morning: Read the six affirmations aloud.
 Evening: Write out the next three affirmations *(Forgiveness - Silver set)* along with previous affirmations. - total nine

Read all nine affirmations.

Start writing your heartfelt vision.

Fall asleep repeating the words, *"I choose to see my worthiness because I exist as a child of God."*

Day Four

Morning: Read the nine affirmations aloud.

Evening: Write out the next three affirmations (*Gratitude - Gems set*) along with previous affirmations. - total 12

Read all twelve affirmations.

Write 5 things of appreciation.

Continue writing your heartfelt vision.

Fall asleep repeating the words, *"I choose to see my worthiness because I exist as a child of God."*

Day Five

Morning: Read the 12 affirmations aloud.

Evening: Write out the next three affirmations (*Courage - Pearls set*) along with previous affirmations. - total 15

Read all 15 affirmations.

Write 5 things of appreciation.

Finish writing your heartfelt vision.

Fall asleep repeating the words, *"I choose to see my worthiness because I exist as a child of God."*

Day Six

Morning: Read the 15 affirmations aloud.

Evening: Write out the next three affirmations (*Faith & Trust - Starfish*) along with previous affirmations. - total 18

Read all 18 affirmations.

Write 5 things of appreciation.

Write the words *"I choose to see my worthiness because I exist as a child of God."* Underneath your appreciation list (*you no longer need to repeat these words before falling asleep*)

Tonight, fall asleep seeing your vision as if it already happened.

Day Seven

Morning: Read the 18 affirmations aloud.
Evening: Write out the next three affirmations (*Self-Empowerment - Gold Doubloons set*) *along with previous affirmations. - total twenty-one*
Write 5 things of appreciation.
Write the words *"I choose to see my worthiness because I exist as a child of God."* Underneath your appreciation list
Read all 21 affirmations.
Fall asleep seeing your vision as if it already happened.

Continue… Daily for the next 21 Days.

Morning: Read the 21 affirmations aloud.
Evening: Write out the 21 affirmations, the 5 things of appreciation and *"I choose to see my worthiness because I exist as a child of God."*
Read all 21 affirmations.
Fall asleep seeing your vision as if it already happened.

ABOUT ANN RUSNAK

Ann Rusnak totally enjoys life, her success and feels great about herself. Ann is passionate about helping determined women entrepreneurs in a supportive, practical way so they can make positive changes about their limiting money.

But there was time when it wasn't so. Ann's parents raised her with the false message there was something wrong with her. She often shares this statement with audiences at her workshops, "My dreams were wrong, and, pursuing a better life was wrong." As a result, she often sabotaged her goals, especially financial ones.

Ann's journey of self-discovery resulted in breaking the cycle of emotional abuse so she could finally step into her own power. She created a new legacy for future generations., by raising an independent, self-assured, self-confident daughter, now a young woman who believes in herself one hundred percent.

She started her own business and quickly was earning six figures. When she became ill, she wisely developed a system where she could keep her business growing and thriving in tiny 15-minutes increments. Then, she sold her unique time management programs to other time-starved, stressed entrepreneurs.

Ann combined her 25 years of business experience and her personal self-discovery journey to create of the powerful 'Unstoppable Success System.' She is excited to share this simple process which empowers women with the clarity and confidence to easily and effortlessly attract more ideal clients.

I didn't feel confident enough to talk to potential clients. Within, two weeks of working with Ann, I shifted my thoughts to be more open especially around money. This resulted in unexpected money showing up and a customer calling me out of the blue to place a big order. I loved how Ann gently guided me to overcome the fear of talking about my business, and to see the worth and value in myself. I'm feeling less stressed and I now attract new clients with confidence. I'm so grateful for all Ann has done.

Rynette Vall

To learn more about how you can work with Ann and to download your "Unstoppable Success Kit: A Simple and Easy Way to Attract Success in Less Than 5 Minutes A Day," go to **www.TheJourneytoMeGift.com**

"I knew I was being way too hard on myself. I needed to get over 'settling' for things that were wrong for me and my business. In the past, I seriously needed validation that I was on the right path. Ann's transformational journey has produced an extensive arsenal of strategies helped me and can help you overcome the inner issues holding you back from experiencing who you're destined to become. She's caring, thoughtful, insightful and helps you get the job done in empowering, rewarding ways. I intend to place more value on who I am and what I offer others. I'm looking forward to sharing my skills and talents through my book, classes and workshops."

Debi Goldben

To invite Ann Rusnak to speak at your upcoming conference or workshop or to explore other ways to work with Ann, visit **www.AnnRusnak.com** or get in touch at 216-941-7059

ACKNOWLEDGEMENTS

This book would not exist without the help, guidance and support of the following people. I cannot thank them enough for the positive impact they have made in my life and I want them to know that I appreciate them with my whole heart.

Family & Friends

To Mike, my wonderful husband: I thank God every day for placing you in my life. Thanks for believing in me, giving me the freedom to express my entrepreneurial calling, and staying by me no matter what. I'm glad you made me a part of your dreams. Thank you for all your help and support with this book. I love you.

To Chantal and Allyce, my loving and beautiful daughters: You taught me how to play, laugh and appreciate what is important in life. You inspired me to become a better person. I couldn't ask for two finer children. I'm so proud of both of you and love you very much.

To my best friend Pat: Where would I be without your friendship, our monthly breakfasts, your letters and words of encouragement and your wisdom? I've enjoyed sharing our life events together over these many years. I truly believe you are my guardian angel.

To Stephanie Rainbow Bell: Who knew attending a business seminar would lead me to meeting somebody who would positively transform my life? Thanks for opening my eyes to living a spirit-led life, showing me the way back to my Magical Essence and being there for me during this incredible journey of inner peace.

To DeLores Pressley: Thank you for writing the forward. I don't know if this book would be a reality without you. It was through your love and support that lead me to realize it's never too late to live my dreams. What a powerful gift you gave me by taking me under your wings, nurturing and encouraging me along the way. I truly appreciate everything you have done and I'm proud and honored to call you my friend.

Mentors and Teachers

To Morgana Rae: You taught me how to finally heal my old stories around money and opened the door to loving myself unconditionally. You transformed my life by putting me on the path to unlimited prosperity and abundance. And on that path, I learned through love to trust, let go and follow my inner guidance. Something I thought would never happen. Thank you.

To Denise Michaels: Looking over the pile of notes, I had compiled for my book, I wondered *How does one begin to write a book*? Since God gave me the idea, He in His wisdom brings the right people and resources at the right time. When you called asking if I wanted to join your new book writing program, how could I refuse? We've known each other since the early internet days, yet it seems like yesterday. I've enjoyed our conversations, your inspiration, mentoring and marketing expertise over the years. I'm forever grateful for your help and encouragement in turning my book dream into a reality. Thank you.

To T.L. Champion: You are a "champion" to the aspiring writer by bringing out their inner author. Thanks for all your encouragement, wisdom, edit suggestions, guidance, and especially, patience. I'm glad you were beside me on this incredible journey to share the tears and laughter along the way. Even though I didn't always agree with you, your input helped to make this book become what I envisioned. I'm proud to be one of your successful author stories.

To Marnie L. Pehrson: Discovering your "She Loves God" writings years ago, allowed me to grow stronger spiritually. You were someone I admired for quite some time and felt honored when God allowed our paths to cross. Thanks for the conversations, wisdom and healings. When an established and bestselling author said she loved this book, it meant so much to me. Your suggestions and edits helped make the story even better and taught me to trust God's timing.

To Jeanna Gabellini: What does a success mindset strategist need when she thinks she has this "Law of Attraction" stuff mastered? Someone to show her she's only getting started. Your mentoring and coaching opened my eyes and mind to greater understanding of the power of allowing. The awakening enabled me to fully step into my power of following divine Magical Essence and taking only inspired action. Living this way makes life so much easier and fun. You Rock!

To Dennis Jarecke: Sometimes you need someone to help you verbalize and translate what is in your brain, so others get it. You are a gifted copywriter and I've enjoyed our journey together, encouraging and sharing stories and resources as we both embarked upon the path of transforming our lives and business. Thank you.

To Mary Lee Boesewetter: Never in a million years did I think receiving a gift certificate for a Reiki session would dramatically change my life in a positive way. You not only healed my body so I could walk the beach again but also healed much of the false beliefs in my mind. Yes, I was skeptical about all this 'science of mind' philosophy, until you seemed to know information about me that I did not share with you. It convinced me to explore and discover how our thoughts create the life we are living. Thanks to your teachings and healing I'm living a much healthier and happier life.

Printed in the United States
By Bookmasters